Evelyn Waugh, Apprentice

Waugh at Oxford, Courtesy of the Harry Ransom Humanities Research Center, the University of Texas at Austin.

Evelyn Waugh, Apprentice

The Early Writings, 1910–1927

**Edited and with an Introduction by
Robert Murray Davis**

Pilgrim Books
Norman, Oklahoma

By Robert Murray Davis

The Novel: Modern Essays in Criticism (Englewood Cliffs, NJ, 1969)
Evelyn Waugh (St. Louis, MO, 1969)
John Steinbeck (Englewood Cliffs, NJ, 1972)
Evelyn Waugh, Writer (Norman, 1981)
Modern British Short Novels (Glenview, IL, 1972)
Evelyn Waugh: A Checklist of Primary and Secondary Material (Troy, NY, 1972)
Donald Barthelme: A Bibliography (Hamden, CT, 1977)
A Catalogue of the Evelyn Waugh Collection at the Humanities Research Center, The University of Texas at Austin (Troy, NY, 1981)
Evelyn Waugh, Apprentice: The Early Writings, 1910–1927 (Norman, 1985)

Library of Congress Cataloging-in-Publication Data

Waugh, Evelyn, 1903–1966.
  Evelyn Waugh, apprentice.

  Includes bibliographies.
  I. Davis, Robert Murray.   II. Title
PR6045.A97A6   1985   823'.912   85–21688
ISBN 0–937664–70–7

Published by Pilgrim Books
P.O. Box 2399, Norman, Oklahoma   73070
Copyright © 1985 by Pilgrim Books
All rights reserved
ISBN: 0–937664–70–7

Printed and bound in the United States of America. First edition.
Waugh materials copyright © by the estate of Evelyn Waugh.

For Donat Gallagher and Winnifred M. Bogaards

Contents

Part Two: The Lancing Years

Part Three: The Oxford Years

Part Four: Becoming a Man of Letters

Appendix: Boiling the Pot and Playing the Poet

Editor's Preface

This volume includes all of the presently available written (as opposed to graphic) juvenile work by Evelyn Waugh not already in print. All of the unpublished material comes from the Evelyn Waugh Collection at the Humanities Research Center, The University of Texas, Austin; the published material is drawn from a variety of sources, many of them unavailable in the United States and most of them not readily accessible in any country.

Spelling and internal punctuation follow, in every case, that of the text cited in the headnotes. Speakers' taglines in the plays and quotation marks have been regularized; no attempt has been made to reproduce the conventional signs used in typescript, since Waugh could not type and therefore did not have control of the text at this stage.

The headnotes to each selection are confined to dating, sources of the texts reprinted, and details of composition except where material is not available in print or where allusions are not self-explanatory.

Works frequently cited are as follows:

Catalogue: Robert Murray Davis. *A Catalogue of the Evelyn Waugh Collection at the Humanities Research Center, The University of Texas at Austin.* Troy, N.Y.: Whitston, 1981.
Diaries: The Diaries of Evelyn Waugh. Edited by Michael Davie. Boston: Little, Brown, 1976.
Letters: The Letters of Evelyn Waugh. Edited by Mark Amory. New Haven, Conn., and New York: Ticknor & Fields, 1980.
A Little Learning: A Little Learning: An Autobiography by Evelyn Waugh. Boston: Little, Brown, 1964.

Other references are given in the headnotes.

The Research Council of the University of Oklahoma provided funds for travel, copying, and research assistance; the staff of the

Evelyn Waugh, Apprentice

Humanities Research Center has, over the past fifteen years, been consistently helpful; and Donat Gallagher, Winnifred Bogaards, and Paul A. Doyle have answered questions and provided photocopies and moral support in this as in other projects. Megan Davis helped prepare the manuscript and read proof.

Norman, Oklahoma   ROBERT MURRAY DAVIS

Editor's Introduction

The precision, wit, and polish evident in Evelyn Waugh's first books, *Rossetti* and *Decline and Fall*, may lead those who do little writing to assume that Waugh's style emerged fully formed and without antecedents. Waugh would have scorned this assumption, even more than, as a man of principle and taste, he deprecated his juvenile work, which he called "quite without interest" and "imitative of the worst of my reading."[1] As the material in this collection demonstrates, he served almost twenty years as an apprentice before publishing his first book.

Much of the material is preserved at the Humanities Research Center of the University of Texas at Austin.[2] Although a great deal has been preserved, even casual persual of Waugh's diaries reveals that considerably more material was not. Furthermore, it is impossible to represent in this volume the youthful Waugh's strong and to his mind paramount interest in the graphic arts. He could draw before he could write, and at Oxford, where he encountered many literary rivals, he was "pre-eminent (for there were no competitors) . . . in making decorative drawings" (*A Little Learning*, p. 189). Moreover, two of his early narratives, "The Slaves of Hurre Len: A Revised Rajah Shoo" and "In Quest of Thomas Lee" (*Catalogue*, A2–3), tell their stores in pictures accompanied by brief captions. The first combines a taste for the exotic with an interest in melodrama and involves the capture of an airplane pilot by a villainous Hindu and a rescue, with danger and surprise improbable enough to satisfy even Princess Jenny Abdul Akbar of *A Handful of Dust*, whose account of her very beautiful and very wicked Moslem husband is probably drawn from the same kind of source. The second deals with the capture by South American natives of the unfortunate Lee and his fortuitous meeting with his brother Christopher

---

[1] *A Little Learning* (Boston: Little, Brown, 1964), pp. 60, 62.
[2] See my *Catalogue of the Evelyn Waugh Collection at the Humanities Research Center, The University of Texas at Austin* (Troy, N.Y.: Whitston, 1981), items G1–2.

1

and his friend Lenard (*sic*), an outcome parallel to but more fortu-
nate than that of *A Handful of Dust*. Except for these anticipations
of later work, however, the drawings of this and of later periods[3]
cannot repay the expense of reproducing them.

The written material has, of course, considerably more value
because it gives evidence of the impulses that pushed him toward
what he came to call the family trade of literature. These were at
least fourfold. First, as he explained in the self-dedication of his
untitled schoolboy novel (selection 19 in this book), he was born
into an intensely literary family in which the writing, reading, and
making of books were regarded as natural if not inevitable activities.
His father, Arthur Waugh, was director of Chapman and Hall, a
solid if not leading publishing firm, and a firmly established if not a
leading reviewer and a man of letters. Moreover, as both Evelyn and
Alec Waugh later testified, much of the social life at the family
home in Hampstead involved literary men, their wives, and occa-
sionally literary women.[4]

A second kind of impetus to authorship came from what would
now be called Evelyn's peer group. With some neighbors, some of
them older, he organized "a patriotic league named The Pistol
Troop," conducted battles with what he called "gutter children"
and later "street cads," and produced a magazine to which adults as
well as children contributed. In less bellicose moods, and without
military sanction, Waugh, the Fleming children (called the Roland
family in *A Little Learning*), and others "produced a number of
plays, written by ourselves and acted in home-made costumes before home-made scenery" (p. 60). Alec Waugh testifies that the
Pistol Troop was succeeded by the "W.U.D.S. (Wyldesmead Underhill Dramatic Society)" and mentions programs, "very professional, . . . illustrated with photographs of the chief performers" (*My
Brother*, p. 168). Two such programs survive at the Humanities
Research Center (*Catalogue*, G1–2). Except for the photographs in
one of the programs, they resemble that given in the notes to "A
Woman's Curse" (selection 5) in casting and in variety of turns.

This kind of activity was probably less rare among children and,
to judge from stories about Arthur Waugh's love of theatrics both
formal and informal, adults than those of us reared with films,

---

[3] See *Catalogue*, sec. H; Alain Blayac, "Evelyn Waugh's Drawings," *Library Chronicle of
the University of Texas*, n.s., no. 7 (Spring, 1974): [42–57]. Blayac reproduces some of the
line drawings.

[4] See Alec Waugh, "Authors at Underhill," in *My Brother Evelyn and Other Portraits*
(New York: Farrar, Straus and Giroux, 1967), chap. 2.

radio, and television can now imagine. Evelyn seems to have dif-
fered from his contemporaries not only in being more talented but,
as his diaries[5] and letters[6] show, in having a strongly competitive
nature.

As early as 1916, when he edited the *Cynic*, he eschewed emula-
tion and, in his opening "Editorial" (selection 9) and manifesto
reprinted below, proclaimed his victory over the official school
magazine. His desire for conflict was premeditated. In a diary entry
for early 1916 not given in *Diaries*, Waugh anticipated the beginning of the winter term at Heath Mount School: "By George when
the term begins things will hum. I think it's my last so I'm going to
raise Hell. Our first shell to smash the ramparts of convention is
'The Cynic' the most gorgeous paper out." In fact, he continued at
Heath Mount until the end of 1916. Issues appeared January 21,
February 8, March 7, May 5, and September. The gap in publication, Waugh explained in the last number, occurred because he was
waiting for a rival paper to appear "so as to deliver some helpful
criticisms to the youthful journalist."

As the "Editorial" indicates, however, the chief object of criticism
was the *Heath Mount Magazine*. Waugh made helpful criticisms of
the masters' efforts and predicted that "when they have had a little
more experience [they] will be able to produce quite a presentable
little paper." Later he apologized for criticizing false rhymes in
comic verse: "Believe me we had no idea it was humourous or we
should have been more lenient."

If the authorities did not actually repress this schoolboy cheek,
they did not encourage it. Waugh noted in his diary that Mr.
Hinchcliffe, his form master, "has of course forbidden the 'Cynic' to
be sold but nevertheless we have already sold out [at threepence
each]. . . . we have after paying for the printing got about halfe a
crown over for the war fund which we are collecting." Later, describing another project, he carefully distinguished between the war
fund and the Waugh fund.

In *A Little Learning*, Waugh gives the impression that his bellicose impulses gave way, about 1915, to the religious period in which
he composed "The World to Come" (selection 15), described as "a
deplorable poem in the metre of Hiawatha . . . describing the experiences of the soul immediately after death" (p. 93). In fact, the

---

[5] *The Diaries of Evelyn Waugh*, ed. Michael Davie (Boston: Little, Brown, 1976).
[6] *The Letters of Evelyn Waugh*, ed. Mark Amory (New Haven, Conn., and New York:
Ticknor & Fields, 1980).

poem must have been composed during the run of the *Cynic*, and Waugh's ability to separate satiric from religious impulses persisted, even more notably in his personal than in his professional life, as long as he lived.

A third impetus to his juvenile writing was his classical and other training at Lancing. Summing up the content and effect of his education in *A Little Learning*, Waugh concluded that "my education . . . was the preparation for one trade only; that of an English prose writer" (p. 140). As Waugh's diaries and relatively few surviving manuscripts demonstrate, public-school boys of that period were asked to do a good deal of writing. Waugh asserted that "our written work was seldom read and then only to criticise style or meaning; spelling was regarded as too elementary for attention" (pp. 139–40), but "Essay" (selection 22) and "The House: An Anti-Climax" (selection 23), preserved by his friend and literary disciple Dudley Carew,[7] demonstrated more careful attention than he recalled. There is no way of knowing whether these were typical responses to assignments, but it is clear from the diaries that Waugh sometimes regarded them as challenges to his ingenuity and to his skill, that he took some pains with them, and that on occasion he sent them to his father and noted, without pain or rancor, even the unfavorable responses.

At least as much energy went into extracurricular writing, some of it officially approved, much of it not. Waugh was acutely, perhaps needlessly, sensitive to the danger of keeping a diary, once destroying part of it and on other occasions exercising prudent self-censorship. He did not give and perhaps did not have a clear motive for keeping it; perhaps he did so because of what he later called the writer's desire to give written shape to his experiences.[8]

A fourth impetus to write was also a result of his recurrent desire to emulate and surpass his brother, Alec. Throughout the period at Lancing College covered by his diaries (September, 1919–December, 1921), visits by Alec, already established as a novelist and man of letters, spurred him to a rivalry that seems not to have been conscious. Perhaps some of the earliest stories and almost

---

[7] See Dudley Carew, *A Fragment of Friendship* (London: Everest Books, 1974).

[8] "Just as a carpenter, I suppose, seeing a piece of rough timber feels an inclination to plane it and square it and put it into shape, so a writer is not really content to leave any experience in the amorphous, haphazard condition in which life presents it; and putting an experience into shape means, for a writer, putting it into a communicable form." *Ninety Two Days* (New York: Farrar and Rinehart, 1934), p. 5.

certainly the schoolboy novel[9] were written with the intention of going his predecessor one better.

There is no question that in "Conversion" (selection 25), a play parodying the maiden-aunt view of school life as well as that of Alec's *The Loom of Youth*, he confronted his older brother head on, for passages in the play are directly traceable to the novel, as the following passages indicate (originally published 1917; I quote the Richards Press edition of 1947):

> "You know I think Meredith goes a bit too far at times," came a voice from the middle of the room.
> Bradford rose at once. "What the hell do you mean? Meredith go too far? Why, he is a splendid wicket-keeper, and far and away the finest half-back in the school. You must allow a good deal to a blood like him."
> "Oh, I know he is a magnificent athlete and all that, but don't you think he does rather a lot of harm in the House?"
> "Harm? Who to?"
> "Well, I mean there's Davenham now and —"
> "Davenham!" came the scornful retort. "What does it matter what happens to Davenham? He's absolutely useless to the House, rotten at games and spends his whole time reading about fossils. . . . Meredith is simply a glorious fellow. Do you remember the way he brought down Freeman in the Two Cock? Why, the House simply couldn't get on without him." [p. 23]

Jeffries has just been expelled, and speaks:

> ". . . it is unfair. Who made me what I am but Fernhurst? Two years ago I came here as innocent as Caruthers there; never knew anything. Fernhurst taught me everything; Fernhurst made me worship games, and think that they alone mattered, and everything else could go to the deuce. . . . And now Fernhurst, that has made me what I am, turns round and says, 'You are not fit to be a member of this great school!' and I have to go. Oh, it's fair, isn't it?" [p. 60]

In a passage too long to quote, Tester, a member of the Sixth form, converts the protagonist to an aesthetic view of life by reading aloud "the great spring Chorus in *Atalanta*, into which Swinburne crowded all that he ever knew of joy and happiness" (pp. 147–49).

Other types of writing (such as speeches prepared for debates or,

---

[9] Waugh called this novel "intolerably bad" in the interview with Julian Jebb, "The Art of Fiction XXX: Evelyn Waugh," *Paris Review* 8 (Summer–Fall 1963): 75. See my essay, "Evelyn Waugh: The Failure of Imagination," *London Magazine*, vol. 25 (April/May 1985), pp. 88–97.

like "The Twilight of Language" [selection 21], for clubs) were equally self-assertive but less obviously bellicose. And, of course, various literary prizes could bring him money—to be spent about equally on books and on food—as well as the regard of masters and contemporaries. He debated often and won several prizes for poems and essays, but only one debate speech is preserved in his diary, and only his prize poem survived in the other materials transmitted to the University of Texas. When Waugh began to pursue the larger prize of an Oxford scholarship in the summer and winter terms of 1921, he abandoned everything but a few debate speeches and editorials for the *Lancing College Magazine*.[10]

Once he reached Oxford, however, he abandoned serious attempts at study and devoted himself to an extensive social life and to various literary projects for undergraduate magazines, including the *Isis*, whose "sole attraction" for Waugh "was that it paid its contributors"; the *Cherwell*, which after an episode with a Philbrickian publisher was financed and edited by Waugh's friends; and the *Oxford Broom*, founded by Harold Acton.

Waugh later regarded his literary contributions as "not . . . much better or much worse than most undergraduate journalism" (*A Little Learning*, p. 187). But he went on to say that one (probably "Edward of Unique Achievement," selection 31) "was a quite funny short story in which an earnest student might find hints of my first novel" and that another ("Antony, Who Sought Things That Were Lost," selection 30) "betrays the unmistakable influence of that preposterously spurious artifact, which quite captivated me at the age of nineteen, James Branch Cabell's *Jurgen*" (*A Little Learning*, p. 189). Those earnest students who read the stories in light of Waugh's juvenilia can see in the contrast between these two stories the split between the anarchic impulses of the *Cynic* and, heavily disguised by melancholy or necromancy, the spiritual impulses of *The World to Come* and between social satire and self-critical justification observable in "The Balance" (selection 36) and in more subtle fashion in *Vile Bodies*.

The undergraduate stories, "The Manager of 'The Kremlin'" (selection 38) and "The Sympathetic Passenger" (selection 41), and, for that matter, most of Waugh's other short stories were mostly written to formula, though that formula changed less because of Waugh's development than because of the audience for whom he

---

[10] Some of this material is reprinted in *The Essays, Articles and Reviews of Evelyn Waugh*, ed. Donat Gallagher (London: Methuen, 1983).

wrote. "The Balance" (selection 36), however, shows Waugh attempting to extend his range both technically and thematically. It was begun while he was teaching in Wales and after he had destroyed "The Temple at Thatch," which "concerned an undergraduate who inherited a property of which nothing was left except an eighteenth-century classical folly where he set up house and, I think, practised black magic" (*A Little Learning*, p. 223). To readers of Waugh's undergraduate stories the themes sound familiar, and there is no evidence that the technique was markedly different. In "The Balance," however, Waugh sought a method by which he could present as objectively as possible material drawn from his own experience. By using cinematic devices, which he had studied as a reviewer of films and in the films which he made with Terence Greenidge and other contemporaries at Oxford, he was able to turn away from the subjectivity which he described in "The Twilight of Language" and was later to condemn in "Ronald Firbank."[11] Moreover, though he used Oxford as a setting, he placed it in the framework of the London social scene which he was to exploit for part of *Decline and Fall*, most of *Vile Bodies*, and in fact most of his mature fiction. And though "The Tutor's Tale: A House of Gentlefolks" (selection 37) was less experimental than "The Balance," it does show the youthful Waugh using the same setting and one of the same characters and thus beginning to create the setting and cast of characters for what came to be called the world of Evelyn Waugh.[12]

Although "The Tutor's Tale" was solicited while Waugh thought of himself as a schoolmaster with literary interests, it was written after he had been fired and had concluded, reluctantly, that "the time has arrived to set about being a man of letters" (*Diaries*, p. 281, February 21, 1927). Technically, one could argue, the period of his juvenilia ends here, or hereabouts. However, the last four items (see Appendix) are included in part because they are not, and are not likely to be, reprinted elsewhere. The poem is a *jeu d'esprit* rare in the life of a writer as professional as Waugh had become, though it can be seen as practice for the sonnet of Ludovic in *Sword of Honour*. The stories, written for immediate gain and apparently not even considered for his collections of stories,[13] show the uses to which Waugh was willing to put his name.

[11] "Ronald Firbank," *Life and Letters* 2 (March, 1929): 191–96.
[12] See my *Evelyn Waugh, Writer* (Norman, Okla.: Pilgrim Books, 1981), pp. 32–37.
[13] Waugh did tell his agent, A. D. Peters, that "The Sympathetic Passenger" might make a good film. See *Catalogue*, E368.

Evelyn Waugh, Apprentice

The material printed for the first time or reprinted in this volume represents rather than exhausts Waugh's juvenile and fugitive work. I have already mentioned the drawings; other material includes poems reprinted in the *Diaries*.[14] *The Essays, Articles and Reviews of Evelyn Waugh*, edited by Donat Gallagher (London: Methuen, 1983), includes fifteen items from Waugh's youthful writings, the story "Consequences," and, of course, a large body of his mature work. Two other uncollected stories, "The Man Who Liked Dickens" and "Compassion," could not be included because they were adapted, respectively, for the climactic episodes of *A Handful of Dust* and *Unconditional Surrender*.

[14] "Ars Amoris for C. F. W.," June 5, 1920; "Lancing Chapel," May 15, 1921, and *A Little Learning*, pp. 141–42; "To a decadent modernist" (titled "To a dilettante" in a separate manuscript, *Catalogue*, B6); "To J[ohn] L[onge] and J. V. H[ale]," June 13, 1921 (Given this title in a separate manuscript, *Catalogue*, B8); "Ode on the Intimations of Immaturity" (for Alec Waugh's birthday), July 8, 1921.

Part One   The Hampstead Years

1

The Curse
of the
Horse Race

[Waugh dates the story as being written in "1910, when I was rising seven," on the basis of the handwriting (*A Little Learning*, p. 62), and reproduces the first page of the manuscript facing p. 15. Text: Manuscript in the Humanities Research Center, *Catalogue* Al. As "The Curse of the Race" in *Little Innocents: Childhood Reminiscences*, by Dame Ethyl Smith and others, Preface by Alan Pryce-Jones (London: Cobden-Sanderson, 1932), pp. 93–96. As "The Curse of the Horse Race" in *Tactical Exercise* (Boston: Little, Brown, 1954); there dated 1910. With same title in *The World of Evelyn Waugh*, ed. Charles J. Rolo (Boston: Little, Brown, 1958).]

CHAP I
BETTING

I bet you 500 pounds I'll win. The speaker was Rupert a man of about 25 he had a dark bushy mistarsh and flashing eyes.

I shouldn't trust to much on your horse said Tom for ineed he had not the sum to spear.

The race was to take place at ten the folowing moring

CHAP II

The next moring Tom took his seat in the grant stand while Rupert mounted Sally (which was his horse) with the others to wate for the pistol shot which would anounse the start.

The race was soon over and Rupet had lost. What was he to do could he do the deed? Yes I'll *kill* him in the night, he thought.

CHAP III
THE FIRE

Rupert crept stedfustly along with out a sound but as he drew his sword it squeeked a little   this awoke Tom seasing a candle he lit it just at that moment Rupert struch and sent the candle flying

The candle lit the cuntain   Rupert trying to get away tumbled over the bed   Tom maid a dash for the dorr and cleided with a perlisman who had come to see what was the matter and a panic took place.

CHAP IIII
EXPLAIND

While Tom and the peliesman were escapeing through the door Rupert was adaping quite a diffrat methand of escape he puld the matris of the bed and hurld [?] the it out of the window then jumped out he landed safe and sound on the matris then began to run for all he was worth now let us leave Rupert and turn to Tom and the peliesman as soon as they got out Tom told the peliesman what had hapend.

CHAP V
HOT ON THE TRAIL

"See there he is" said Tom "We must folow him and take him to prizen" said the peliesman.

There's no time to spere said Tom letts get horses said the peliesman so they bort horses and and galerpin in the direcion they had seen him go.

On they went aintil they were face to face with each other. the peliesman lept from his horse only to be stabed to the hart by Rupert then Tom jumped down and got Rupert a smart blow on the cheak.

CHAP VI
A DEADLY FIGHT

This enraged Rupert thake [*sic*] that he shouted and made a plung but tom was too quick for him artfully dogeing the sword he brout his sword round on Rupert's other cheak.

Just at that moment Ruper slashed killed the peliesmans horse then lept on Toms horse and galapt off.

CHAP VII
THE MYSTERIOUS MAN

Of cause then was no chance of catching him on foot so Tom walked to the nearest inn to stay the night but it was ful up he had to share with a nother man.

Thou Tom was yerry tired he could not sleep, their was something about the man he was he did not like he reminded him of some one he didnot know who. Sudnly he felt something moveing on the bed looking up he saw the man fully dressed just getting off the bed.

CHAP VIII
RUN TO ERTH

Now Tom could see that the mysteraous man was Rupert. Has he come to do a merder? Or has he only come to stay the night? thees were the thoughts that rushed throu Toms head he lay still to what Rupert would do first he opened a cubord and took out a small letter bag from this he took some thing wich made Toms blod turn cold it was a bistol Tom lept forward and seesed Rubert by [?] the throught and flung him to the ground then snaching a bit of robe from the ground he bound Rupert hand and foot.

CHAP IX
HUNG

Then Tom drest himself then Tom took Rupert to the puliese cort Rupert was hung for killing the pulies man. I hope this story will be aleson to you never to bet.

[Undated. The handwriting is better formed than that of "Race" but is less sophisticated than that of "Told by the Refuggee," but more exact dating between 1910 and 1914 is not possible. Text: Manuscript in the Humanities Research Center, *Catalogue*, A4.]

CHAPTER I

Midnight boomed from the old clock tower and still the two men played on. Ralfe the eldest son of Gerald Cantonville had got in debt to a villainous money lender and in desperation had taken to gambling in a great efort to "raise the wind" all in vain on he played and still Baycraw won. Sudenly the door opened and in came a young boy of nineteen he had just left his public school carrying away nearly every cup at the sports. He was certainly not clever clever [*sic*] for he had never got any higher than the upper fifth   "Hullo Ralfe still playing I should turn in"   The elder brother looked up sharply "Get off to bed youngster" he growled and then returned to the game. Tom Cantonville shrugged his shoulders and went out with despair in his heart

Baycraw tiptoed down stairs and opened the window a cold draft of air blew in. He wistled softly and a dark form was siluetted for a moment against the bleu without. Then came a soft thud and a wispered warning. Then silence. The two men Baycraw and Fidon crept up stairs and having opened the door Mr. Cantonville's room switched on the light. The old man turned over binked and started only to find himselfe looking down the barrel of a "colt" revolver
    "Make a sound and your a dead man" wispered Braycow [*sic*]
    "Who are you" murmered the terrified man
    "You know very well! You havn't such a bad memory as all that. Come no think can't remember a certain bank robbery in which a

certain Cargon figurgered, do you not recall what he said when you found him out eh? something about revenge? well I am he and this—Fidon at this moment broke off as Braycaw raising a knife plunged it down ward there was a strangled and stilness.

"This" continued Fidon "Is our revenge

CHAPTER II

Halfe past eight and stil no apearance of Mr. Cantonville. They began to get nervous he was always punctual. Tom went to see what it was. In a minute he staggered back white to the lips his hand on his fore head he reeled into a chair and lay their like one dead his breath coming in short gasps Ralfe ran to the side bord and returned with a liqure glass of brandy. Tom drunk it and sat up "He's dead" he said "they bloods all over his chest. Mrs. Cantonville rushed up to the room followed by all the other. There lay Mr. Cantonville a knife embedded in his chest. "We'd better leave it as it is for the detectives to see" advised Ralfe   Tom was already at the telephone and in ten minutes a car swung up the drive and a detective alighted. All this time Braycaw was sitting in the breakfast room puffing a segar but now he followed the detective to the scene of the crime. The detective bent out of the boddy and drew out the knife it was an Idian dagger which had belonged to Ralfe but which he had given as security to Braycaw on not being able to pay for the gambling. "Why" cried Barbarous his sister "That's Ralfe's knife"

the detective turned on Ralfe   "Can you acount for this?" he demanded

"I think I can" said Braycaw stepping forward   "He was in debt and he was heir to all his father's property and money

"You cad" cried Ralfe leaping forward but was brough up by the detectives revolver leveled at him

"Mr Ralfe Cantonville" he said dryly "you can make all your excuses in court untill then consider yourselfe under arest."

Tom buried his face in his hands. He heard a click and saw Ralfe handcuffed. He turned and ran down stairs and buring his face in his hands sobbed like a child. Suddenly the door swung open and in walked Braycaw a cynical smile on his lips   Tom leapt to his feet his eyes blazing   "Rather unfortunate about your brother eh? what?" drawled Braycaw. Tom's reply was a terific swing of his fist. Braycaw who was not a big man stagered back his hands on his face and colapsed on the floor. Tom turned on his heel and left the room leaving Braycaw in a heap on the ground with a broken nose.

CHAPTER III

Now what ever falts Fidon might have he was not a cad and upon hearing of Ralfes arrest he quicly resolved to turn kings evidence and so it was that at halfe past five that evening there was a knock at the door and a clean shaven made [*sic*] steped into the spaceous hall of Cantonville Chase. He was ushered into the drawing room where he found Tom dedjectedly trying to read. He came quicly to the point and told everything. Tom escitedly brought paper and pen and the confetion was written. Sudenly there came a report the smashing of glass and a cry from Fidon a small figure rushed in flung some thing on the ground and the whole room was full of smoke. Tom stagered to the window and let in a cool draft of night air. As smoke cleared away he saw Fidon lying with a bullet in his head and the precious confetion was gone. Then he heard the purr of a motor car outside he rushed only to see Braycaw in a motor disapearing outside he seize his bike and in a second was following. On and on they went in a mad chase the result of which would mean a mans life Tom drew his "Browning" revolver and fire into the darkness ahead he fired again and saw a jet of flame shoot out of the car. he had fired the petrol! the car lurched and swurved; a dark form lept from it. Tom jumped from his bike and seized Braycaw by the coat. A swift turn and Braycaw was gone leaving Tom holding the coat. But Tom could see in the light of the blazing car something that made his heart leap with joy-out of the pocket petruded the confetion. Ralfe was safe!

CHAPTER IV

The light streamed in at the window and Tom sat up his first action was to feel under the pillow and a sigh of relief broke from his lips as he felt the paper but he must get on the trial was tomorro and he had a long way to go. He looked at the clockit was 10 o'clock in 24 hours the trial would take place. He dressed and after a hasty meal hurried to the station the train was waiting and he got in. Five minutes later the train had started and was just getting up steam when a bearded gentleman rushed up the platform and leapt at the train. With agility that did not suite his years he swung onto the footbord and so in to the window where Tom was seated. Having apologies for his strange entrance he settled down and to all ap- earances slept   Tom looked him up and down and noticed he had a broken nose. He began to suspect something. He sliped his hand behind the visitor and pulled one of the locks and he saw it was a wig. Then he lept forward and seized the beared it came away in his hand revealing Braycaw who leapt at him. The two struggled feercly together for some time then as they realed against the door it gave and they fell out on the hill down which the roled until it came to are [?] shere drop Tom lost contitiousness

When Tom recovered his senses it was dark he felt in his pocett and struck a light he was lying on a bush petruding from the side. Braycaw had been caught in the bush also but by his neck and he lay dead   Tom shuddered. But he had other thinks than a murderer's fate to trouble his mind. In a few hours his brother would be tried and he must get there with the confetion. He looked about him and saw the only possible way to escape was by most dangerous and wll nigh imposible climb. But he saw that if he was to save his brother he must act and act quicly slowly raised himselfe to a stanidng possition then he felt above him and gripped the rock above slowly he puled himselfe up and then he found himselfe looking into a cave. He then remembered that it was a sumuggler's cave that led to the old inn. He made his way up and opened the trap door which opened into the inn yard he pulled himselfe up and then began the race against time he rushed to the station just as the train was starting and leapt to the footboard of the engin   "Would you like to earn a five pound note and save a man's life" he cried   The man looked amazed "Then reach Sherborough before ten" that was all. The driver opened the throttle of the engine and she sped forward into the night

CHAPTER V

Nine o'clock struck and Ralfe paced his sell restlesly   He put his hand to his hot head "could it be true? or was only a dreadful nightmare?" he flung himselfe on the hard bench "What if the trial did go against him? hung" he shuddered there was one window in his sell a small grating he could not escape.

Ralfe clung to the rail of the box as one witness after another rose and then suddenly there staggered into the room a young man his colar undone his tie twisted and blood on his face a bandage round his head. it was Tom. It is needless to desscribe the whole trial. Let it be said only that Tom's arival saved Ralfe who was aquitted "without a stain on his character. Now he has a pretty wife and two children and often on Autumn evening they sit round the fire never tiered of following with their father his adventures and those of his brother in the race against time to get Fidon's confetion.

The End

3   *Multa Pecunia*

[The text is that of *The Pistol Troop Magazine*, 1912, pp. 1–6. Waugh edited the magazine. For his comments on the troop, the magazine, and his own contribution— "a story of hidden treasure . . . quite without interest"—see *A Little Learning*, pp. 59–60. For a discussion of anti-German sentiment which led to the founding of the troop, see Christopher Sykes, *Evelyn Waugh: A Biography* (Boston: Little, Brown, 1975), pp. 14–15.]

CHAPTER I

Sir Alfred James, a great collector of books, one day chanced to look at an old volume which had the curious name of "Multa Pecunia," which told him that under his house there was a cave in which was untold of wealth. He did not trouble to read any more, for he had heard the yarn before, and did not believe it.

When Tom came home, being Sir Alfred's son, he was treated with great respect by the servants and therefore was allowed to go into every nook and corner of the house. He was in a little poky room one day, when he saw this carving "Multa Pecunia." He stared for some time at the carving, when suddenly he remembered seeing a book in the library with the same title. Immediately he ran to the library and took out the catalogue. There he saw these words, "Multa Pecunia, shelf 7, place 13." He was immediately at shelf 7, but place 13 was empty!

CHAPTER II

What could it mean? Why had the book gone? He was quite bewildered. "Jumping Golliwogs" cried Tom at last, "I must tell the Pater." He left the room with the intention of going to tell his father about the mysterious disappearance of the old volume; perhaps his father had it, or—Hark! what was that! the rustling of stiff paper was audible. He was now quite close to Smith, the butler's room. The door was open so he looked in. There he saw Smith leaning over the old volume deeply engrossed. Suddenly he got up and walked stealthily to the door. Then he walked off in the direction of the room with the carving. When he got there he pressed the letter "U" and immediately a little trap door opened which was about 17 by 13 inches. Into this crept Smith followed by Tom. The two crept along a passage, and stopped at the sight of a great granite door. "Smith! what does this mean?" cried Tom putting his hand on Smith's collar. Smith fairly staggered when he saw Tom; in fact he simply lost his head, and flew at Tom's throat. A tremendous fight ensued in which Tom with his knowledge of boxing gave him, gave Smith an "up shot" blow that fairly staggered him. But in the end weight won and Tom was knocked senseless to the ground: but Smith was not a fellow to leave him there, he carried him up the steps and laying him down at the door of the library, then closing the door of the secret cave, and putting back the old volume in the library as he found it, he went back to bed.

Sir Alfred came striding along the passage to the library when he suddenly stopped in utter astonishment. "Tom!" he gasped as he saw the boy's pale face.

CHAPTER III

When Tom came to consciousness he found himself in a soft feather bed with a nurse at his bedside. "Ah! that's good, he is conscious now" she whispered. "Why did Smith attack me? asked Tom feebly. "He's delirious" said the nurse turning to the doctor, "I thought he would be after that fall, poor boy"; for the library being at the foot of a flight of steps, Sir Alfred and the nurse naturally thought he had fallen down them.

A long time had past and Tom had not been allowed to see anyone as he had concussion of the brain. At last he was allowed to see someone and nurse asked him who he would choose for his first visitor. "Smith" was the reply. In came Smith very shyly. Why did you fling me down on that stone" demanded Tom.

CHAPTER IV

Now Smith was not usually a butler. He was really a proffesional thief and so he soon thought of what to say, so turning to the nurse he said "I think I had better go for the excitement of seeing anybody after such a long time of quiet has made him a bit mad," with that he left the room.

Tom was quite well and able to run about the house, so he thought he would see Smith. Smith was not in his room, so Tom thought that he would go into the secret cave. He went to the old carving, pressed the letter "U," immediately the same door opened. He went along the passage. Suddenly he stopped abruptly, for footsteps could be heard coming towards him. He crouched down waiting ready to spring. The footsteps came nearer and nearer. Tom could feel his heart thumping against his ribs. Suddenly appeared round the corner of the passage, Tom was on his in a minute and taken by surprise Smith was flung senseless to the ground. Tom was just getting up when he saw a piece of old parchment, he opened it and this is what he read — "I, Wilfred James have stolen these articles of great price from Queen Elizabeth. I could not keep the secret so I put my confidence in Sir Walter Raleigh who gave a hint about it to the great statesman Bacon, who told Queen Elizabeth. The troops of soldiers will be here in one hour and if they find the jewels I shall be locked in the Tower." There the paper ended, so Tom began to look for the jewels, and found them in Smith's pocket. Then putting Smith back on his bed he went to his father's study and told Sir Alfred all the paper had said, and showed him the jewels.

The next day Sir Alfred gave Smith the "sack" and the day after he was found to be the worst thief that ever puzzled Scotland Yard and was arrested and sent to Dartmoor convict prison.

The End

4 *The Sheriff's Daughter or In Parker's Ranche*

[This is probably the earliest surviving example of a play written for performance by Waugh and his friends in Hampstead. Although the manuscript is undated, the handwriting seems to indicate that it was written not too long after "Fidon"; it can tentatively be assigned to 1913. Text: Manuscript in the Humanities Research Center, *Catalogue,* B2.]

Act one

Scene outside Sheriff's house log shanty to right of stage mountain back ground with mining shantes dotted about. Ciril found gazing at notice on log Shanty

Ciril.   I'm a detective don't you know
But out here its awfully slow
So now its come I'll willingly show
Every thing I jolly well know
    Don't you know
    Don't you know
    Don't you know.

The Sheriff's daughter enters from right a group of cowboys from left.

Chorus.   Shut your jaw you silly ass
can't you see the Sheriffs lass
You silly ass, shut your jaw
For there's young Jack in yonder door
See he holds a bunch of roses
Nows the time which he prepose[s?]
silly ass shut your jaw
you're just a silly, ugly bore

Jack.   Come, Come to me my fair and beatious dove

For though a common cowboy I can love
As much a[s] all the haughty earls
Who say that comon men should marry comon girls
Marrey me; do!!
Although a comon cowboy I will fight
Better than any crafty swordsman for the right
And 'though my manner may be some-what plain
Although I've struggled with myself I can't refrain
From loving you
Although your father makes me slave
I swaer to you I'll slay the man who'll brave
To take before my very eyes may wife
He who does this will pay me with his life
    'Tis only true.

Celia.   How can I tell that you are realy brave
Supose someboddy's life you were to save
Then I would marry you — but now I deem
I have a really useful scheme
I'll prove that your talk isn't only bluff
By wedding he, who captures El Maduff

Ciril (timidly).   but what if we all do

Celia.   Be quiet you or there will be a spill
Now I'll depart, for I have said my will

exit

Chorus.   Celia will be my bride
So you lot needn't put on side
For you will be on a very branch
When I walk off with the beau of the ranche

Ciril.   The whole ranche cannot have one wife
It's sure to end in silly strife
In which there may be loss of life
   Why not leave her to me?

Chorus.   Or me?

Jack.   Why waste ye time in silly talk
Up yonder mountain side I now will walk
To chivey El Maduff until he dies
For in his death my future hapiness now lies

(All this time he has been loding his rifle now he straitens up)

Exit

Chorus.   To kill this outlaw we will try
  We'll capture El Maduff or die

Ciril.   I shouldn't do that for if you did only one man would
  remain in the range

Chorus.   Of coare that was only poeticle

Curtain

End of Act One

The Sheriffs Daughter

By E. Waugh
A Comic Operor in the State of Bancerneigh

Act II
or
In Parker's Ranche

Act two

Scene   mountain pass. Professor Lazmouse found escamining
specimen box

Prof. Laz.   I tramp and tramp 'till my legs ache with cramp
  And havn't a specimen yet
  As soon as I get 'em
  Although I don't let 'em
  The escape through without [?] let
    you Bet
    you Bet

Enter El Maduff

El Maduff.   A notorious outlaw is my trade
  It used to suit me very well
  A lot of money have I made
  But now I'm in a beastly sell
  All Parker's ranche is on my track
  I am 'cert to get caught in the end
  Of faith and courage I don't lack
  But there's nowhere for help to send.

Prof. Laz.   Can I oblige—my card *(fumbles in his pocket. El*
  Maduff quietly steals his specimen box)

24

The Sheriff's Daughter or In Parker's Ranche

El Maduff.   I think that I will go now *(beetle crawls out of box onto his had)*   help! what is it? take it away! *(rushes out)*

Enter Cowboys

Ciril.   There he is! quick! after him!

Prof. Laz.   Can I oblige — Oh what the —

Chorus.   Got you! I marry Celia!!

Ciril.   Hullo Jack has vanished!

scene two

Back of log shanty. Gallows arrected. Celia found crying.

Celia.   Oh dear! my heart is broken
  I knew Jack loved me
  Why did I want a token
  O foolish love, thou'st killed me
  I cannot live with Ciril
  I render up my life to thee

(raises revolver)

Jack.   Hold!!! Rash woman
  I am your bride
  Do not marry Ciril for he lied
  I have captured El Maduff
  Am I not brave enough
  To marry you.

Celia.   Of course

Enter Ciril

Ciril.   Ah Jack has returned. I hope you know that I have captured El Maduff.

Jack.   False man! thou lied
  In orer that you might obtain a bride
  I saw 'twas El Maduff who fled
  Therefore I have the honour of this lovely bride
  to wed.

Enter Cowboys

Chorus (jeering).   We see you have returned in time to see El Maduff hung.

Jack.   On the contrary I have arrived arrived in time to set Proffessor Lazmouse B.A.H.C.B.H.G. free

Evelyn Waugh, Apprentice

Chorus.   What do you mean

Enter El Maduff and Prof. Laz (with bound hands led by cowboys)

Cowboys.   Come let us have a trial
  In the true cowboy style
  For all our documents of law
  Say that this case must end in war
  Although this custom's old and cruel
  We've got to end it in a duel

Ciril.   I think I'd rath not
  For Jack's the better shot
  I'll leave to him my wife
  Rather than risk my life
  So now to Celia and the rance adiu
  For I must go if I can't marry you

Prof. Laz.   Oh don't say that for you're still yound
  Don't be so ready with shard [?] yoy [?] tongue
  For now in yonder tent there lies
  My daughter who's about your size
    Why not marry her

El Maduff.   I[t] says in your cowboy law
  That an outlaw cannot be led
  To the gallows, or even shot dead
  When more than one couple is wed
  So now I'm free to sore
  out of your prison door.

Chorus.   So now he's free to sore
  out of our prison door
  It says so in our law

Jack.   Adiu, Adiu   Oh El Maduff
  Once I was poor but now I've enough
  In Parkers Ranche a lot you've done
  But best of all my girl you've won

enter Sheriff

Sheriff.   I think I can oblige you with a wife
  Who'll serve you well and kindly [?] all your life
    My younger daughter

enter Catherine

The Sheriff's Daughter or In Parker's Ranche

Catherine.   I love you for you're strong and fine
  You are the man for whom I used to pine

Exeut (dancing)

Chorus.   Three couples are married today
  But Jack's is the happiest one we'll lay
  For as an under Sheriff he'll stay
  And a right good sheriff who may
  Become the Sheriff of Bancercheigh

Curtain

[In a diary entry of 1914 (*Catalogue*, D7), not reproduced in *Diaries*, Waugh reproduced the "Programme," probably given on Saturday, September 19:

    I War News
    II A Woman Curse
    III Sharing Mat[?]h
    IIII Charade

Waugh comments that "The 'Woman Curse' was the star thing on which I had spent 6 shillings and it went finely[?]. I was Tse Fing." Text: Carbon typescript in the Humanities Research Center, *Catalogue*, B1.]

People

Harper   *The British Minister*
Violet   *His Daughter*
Tse Fing
A Chinese Mandarin

        Scene: Shang-Hai, China.

Act I

Room of English Police Embassy at Shang-Hai. Harper is seated at desk. Looks at watch.

Harper.   I wish Tse Fing would hurry up, he's hardly ever late.

        (Enter Tse Fing)

Tse Fing.   What hast thou called me for, *me*, a Mandarin?

Harper.   I want to know if you can sell up . . .

(Enter Violet)

Violet (Excitedly).   Mr. Carthways has been murdered by the Red Hand *(Tse Fing starts)* while he was at Dinner.

Harper.   Good Heavens! This is getting too bad! Englishmen being murdered! I was just going to issue this order *(Takes paper up)* Take it over to the Station at Washan and have it issued.

Violet.   You might translate it to me, you know I can't read the bestly language.

Harper.   All right: — "There will be given to anyone man, woman, or child the sum of 1,000 dollars if he (or she) can give information as to the heads of the Red Hand." What d'you think o' that? If anything will move these Coolies, its money.

Violet.   All right *(taking up paper)* Good-bye *(Steps towards the door)*.

Tse Fing.   Stop! *(Steps in front of door)* Thou art doing things about which thou knowest nothing.

Violet.   *(Icily)* Do you mind moving away from the door?

(Exit)

Tse Fing.   Call back the cub!

Harper.   And if I don't?

Tse Fing.   You will feel the clutch of the Red Hand.

Harper.   I don't care. Let your Red Hand do its worst.

Tse Fing.   *(Muttering)* Rash words, very rash words. It may be worth your while to recall them. *(Exit just outside the door)* Rash words. We will see.

(Crash outside)

Harper.   Good Lord! What's that?

(Enter Violet, blood running down her face.)

What the . . . ?

Violet.   A tile was thrown from the roof of one of the houses.

Harper.   Are you hurt?

Violet.   I've scratched my face rather badly.

Harper.   Best go into Mathers's next door. He knows first aid.
  (She exits)

  (Scream outside)

Harper.   Violet! Why she's not there.

  (A Red Hand flutters in at the door.)

Harper.   Good Lord! The Red Hand!!!

Curtain

Act II

Tse Fing's house. Tse Fing discovered lying on a matress fanning himself.

Tse Fing.   She certainly is very pretty, but she knows too much.
  I must guard her. Ah . . .

(Shots heard outside, enter Harper with revolver in his hand)

Tse Fing.   Rather an unseemly entrance, don't you think?
  (Harper covers him with revolver) Put that silly thing away.

Harper.   Now you dog, I want my daughter.

Tse Fing.   Then I should put that revolver away.

Harper.   And why?

Tse Fing.   For the simple reason that by striking this gong, thy
  daughter dies.

Harper.   You cur.

Tse Fing.   I want to ask you a question. Will you consent to my
  marriage with your daughter? I meant to kill her, but I love
  her now.

Harper.   Married to *you*! I'd rather die.

Tse Fing.   Then she'll die *(Raises sword)*

  (Enter Violet)

Violet.   Stop!

Tse Fing.   Why so cross my darling? *(sheaths sword)*.

Violet.   I'm not your darling.

Tse Fing.   Nay, cool thy temper and drink tea.

(They sit down together. Tse Fing pours something into Harper's cup)

Tse Fing. There have been many unsolved mysteries in China *(drinks tea)* there will be another added.

Harper. What do you mean?

Tse Fing. Your disappearance *(To Violet)* Now thou shalt see thy father die. *(Raises hammer of gong)*

Violet. Heaven curse you, dog!

Tse Fing. You... You... *(takes Harper's cup and drinks)* Oh! cruel fate. *(Dies).*

Harper. I think this will be an end of the Red Hand. All through your curse. *A Woman's Curse!*

Curtain

6 *Why Britain Is at War*

[Undated, but internal evidence indicates that these lines were written shortly after the beginning of World War I (August 4, 1914), perhaps before "A Woman's Curse." Text: Manuscript in the Humanities Research Center, *Catalogue,* C1.]

When Britain pledged her word there no need for scraps of paper. Britain kept her word. She swore to protect Belgium's neutrality and when the Prussian breaking all treat[ys?] invaded her we then and not ill then joined in. Befor we had only promised to gaurd Frances North Sea ports. I was a good thing that we joined in for if we had we should soon have been envaded.

For Germans toast the day but now it is come they do not like. They never counted on Ulster proving loyal!

7

Told by the Refuggee

[Internal evidence indicates that this piece was written in the fall of 1914, probably before "Come to the Coach House Door." Text: Manuscript in the Humanities Research Center, *Catalogue*, A5.]

M. Lébouge and his wife were happy — so happy. They had bought their little cottage outside Antwerp just that year and had planted their little cabbage patch. All was sunny in Flanders yesterday. Today has come — *The* day has arrived and the black cloud of war has swept over this pleasant cottage and its occupants. The Vandal Hun reeks his awfull vengeance on this brave nation. Slowly he pushes on untill the great bombardment comes and then. The first shell strikes the roofe from that little cottage which [?] only yesterday was someons home. Mme. and her husband rush out and even as they run a shellbursts behind them Mme runs on blindly but M. Lébouge turning to view his home for the last time in this world falls forward a mass of helpless clay. Turned once again into the dust from which he came to satisfy the invaders thirst for blood. The sequel to this small sketch is even worse than the first. In a large reffugee home sits disconsilatly the wreck of a once beautiful women: all in this world is lost to her. When you enter she looks up expectantly as if seeking the tread never to be heard again in this world. But on the morro that is soon to dawn for every one such case will treble toll be taken

8

Come to the Coach House Door, Boys

[The copy is undated, but it is typed and bound in the same format as "A Woman's Curse" and thus very roughly contemporary with it. Since a fake zeppelin attack figures prominently and the first raid on London took place on May 31, 1915, mid-1915 can be conjectured. Text: Carbon typescript in the Humanities Research Center, *Catalogue*, B3.]

Dramatis Personae

Mrs. Malaher
Mr. Malaher
David Malaher

Act I . . . Scene 1. Dave's Bedroom
         Scene 2. Outside Coach House

Act II . . .   Malaher's Dining Room

Act I

Scene 1. David's Bedroom. David found in pyjamas.

David.   Fine is the clan of Malahers; of Scotch descent are we
     Whether in peace or war time, we are the first to flee
     We ran away at Bannockburn, we fled at Flodden field
     In fact in every fight we are the very first to yield
     I'd keep our reputation up if I was at the war
     I'd soon run back right to the base if I was in the fore.

(Enter Mrs. Malaher)

Mrs. Mal.   Now David lift your eyes and look up to the sky.

(He goes to window)

David.   Oh mother go and call papa, a Zeppellin I spy.

(Enter Mr. Malaher)

Mr. Mal.   Hush, hush, my dear. No cause for fright,
  I'm all prepared, it's quite all right,
  Have either of you got a light?
  The wind is blowing hard to-night.

Mrs. Mal.   Oh marvellous man!
  What is the plan?

Mr. Mal.   Make less noise than even a mouse
  As you follow me down to the coach house.

David.   And please remember while descending
  That the 15th stair is wanting mending.

Chorus.   *(Link arms)*
  Malahers we the dauntless three
  Descend the stair with utmost care.

David.   Oh Mother dear I call this bliss,
  Both music & reading I now shall miss.

(Exeunt)

Scene 2
Outside coach house
Enter Mr. & Mrs. Malaher & David

Chorus.   Everyone else may go to their grave
  But whatever comes ourselves we'll save.

(David tries to open door with no result)

David.   Oh mother dear what putrid luck
  The horrid nasty door has stuck.

Mr. Mal.   That *I* can do it I have no doubt
  It opens inward from without.

(David pushes while his father pulls. Mrs. Malaher faints)

Mrs. Mal.   This silly nonsense no must stop,
  We'll have to get in through the top.
                (Exeunt. Door swings open)
                (Great hammering outside)

Voice of Mrs. M.   I've made a whole.

Voice of David.   And I a rent.

Voice of Mr. Mal.   It's easy work cutting cement.

Voice of Mrs. M.   You jump first.

Voice of Mr. M. Ladies first my dear.

Voice of Mrs. M. You go dear David.

Voice of David. No Mother.

Voice of Mr. M. Go!

Voice of David. Oh!

(Crash)

Voice of David. Oh, ow, oh, ohoooooooreeeee.

Voice of Mr. M. *(Showing light down, revealing David seated on a smashed bicycle.* What's the matter? Please don't yelp.

David. Help! Murder! Murder! Help!

Mrs. M. I'll jump down and see what's wrong.

Mr. M. Daylight won't be long.

Mrs. M. You jump too.

Mr. & Mrs. M. 1, 2, 3, . . . *(Crash)*

Mr. M. I've broken my leg, I'm sure.

Mrs. M. Oh dear, oh help, oh lor'.

(Day dawns)

David. The day is dawning!
  Here comes the morning!

Chorus. Through the dark hours of mystery and dread
  When we should have been snuggled up in bed
  Out in the night air we wept
  When if we'd stayed in doors we should have slept.

Mr. & Mrs. Mal. Where's the Zeppellin.

David. There was not an airship mother dear
  There really is no need for fear.

Mrs. Mal. There never was an aircraft seen?
  What d'you mean? Oh, what d'you mean?

David. To miss my music lesson I strived
  So this lovely plan I then contrived.

(Exit)
(Mr. Malaher chases with slipper in hand)

Act II

Scene: Dining Room of Malaher's
    Next morning, Mrs. Malaher found weeping.

Mrs. Mal.   A deal of money we have lost
    Cemented roofs a fortune cost
    And all through naughty wicked Dave
    I'll beat him black and blue the knave.

(*Enter Mr. Malaher, shoe in hand*)

Mr. Mal.   I'm sorry dear that I am late
    My son I've had to chastigate.

(*Yells outside*)

Mrs. Mal.   But does he know why you're so cross?

Mr. Mal.   I told him all about our loss.

Voice at door.   Please mam (*sob*) man [for may?] I c-c-c-ome in?

Mrs. Mal.   Do you really repent you sir?

David.   Yes. (*Sob*)

Mrs. Mal.   Then come in remember please...

David.   But mother dear I've got a weeze.

(*Enter*)

Mrs. Mal.   What's that about?

Mr. Mal.   Spit it out.

(*They crowd together & whisper*)

Mr. Mal.   (at telephone)
    Is that three, eight, six, 1, 0, naught?
    Send someone down that he may report,
    The damage done us by a shell
    That's all, thank you, ring the bell. (*rings*)

Mrs. Mal.   The whole in the wall is big enough,
    I don't think that he'll need much bluff.

(*Knock at door, exit Mr. Malaher*)

Mrs. Mal.   He'll know how he's been had some day
    No hostile aircraft came our way.

David.   He's drawing pictures of the smash
    He's now examining the gash.

Mrs. Mal.   He's coming in now do let's hide.

(Exit)

David.   I say, he can't half put on side.

(dives under table)

Mr. Mal.   Ha! Ha! Ho! Ho! *(pulls out bank notes and huge piece of paper)*

Mr. Mal.   *(reading)*
Awful wreck at Golders Green
Worst smash ever seen
Little boy's heroic act
Coach house roof dreadf'ly cracked.

(Smothered giggles from under table)
(Exit Mr. Malaher)

Voices outside: Yes, that's all right, good day.

(Enter Mr. & Mrs. Malaher, David gets out from under table and they link arms)

Chorus.   Malahers we the dauntless three
Get our share foul or fair
We always score with laughter roar
Ho, ho, hee, hee, he, heeeeeeeee!

Curtain

From *The Cynic*

[The material below is reprinted from the five mimeographed issues of the magazine, the only copies recorded, in the Humanities Research Center. For a discussion of Waugh's editorship, see the Introduction.]

Volume I, No. I January 21st. 1916

9
The Cynic
Cynical Without Being Cheaply So
Piquant in Moderation
Racy in Excess

Editorial

With all hopes for a large sale we set forward this our first number of the "Cynic." It is intended to set out the views of the School rather than those of the masters as is the case with the "Heath Mount Magazine" which it is compulsory to buy, and therefore, much less appreciated.

N.B. We are not trying to excel our contemporary, we *have* excelled it.

The Editor.

Volume I, no. 3.

10
In Our Doggerel Depot
Ode to Sixayitis

There was a small boy at Heath Mount
With questions too many to count

> I've heard people say
> He's not stopped for a day
> And it's perfectly true I've no doubt.
>   (With apologies for the bad rhyme.)

E. W.

11   *To a Latin Prose*

> I took it up my face was glad
> That master wrote 3 — very bad
> When I returned my face was sad
> — — — — — — —

I'D MADE A ROUGH COPY WHAT'S MORE.

E. W.

Volume I, No. 4, May 5th. 1916

12   *Sufficient unto the Day or*
The Importance of Being Lazy

Dramatis Personae

Swotfond	*A hardworking lad.*
Jenkins	*Not a hard working lad.*
Mr. West	*A master*
Mr. Greenfield	*A Head Master*
Catt	*Head Prefect*

Members of the first, second and third forms.

The scene is in the middle school room, time 8-55. The clock on the wall, following the time honoured custom of Heath Mount clocks remains at 4-37 during the whole play. It is Monday morning.

Catt.   I say I've got a tricky question in the latin grammar. What's "Dido driven wild by the horrible designs

1st Second Former.   "Dido coeptis imanibus effena," I suppose.

Catt.   That's funny. You're the first chap to get that right, but you see me get the fellows. I say Smith, d'you know the Latin?

2nd S.F.   'Course not. *(resumes his conversation)*

Catt. Well what's "Dido driven wild by her horrible designs?"

2nd S.F. What's that you say? Oh, "dido coeptis imanibus effena" of course.

Catt. By George, you're the first fellow who's got that right. *(Bell rings.)*

2nd S.F. There's the bell.

Catt. *(Going into the gym with 3rd S.F.)* By the way what's "Dido driven wild by her horrible designs"?

3rd S.F. "Dido coeptis imanibus effena." Why?

Catt. Well you're the first chap who's got it right.

(exeunt.)

Small Kid. Cave *(Exit all)*

Mr. Greenfield, Mr. West & other masters cross the gym.

All. *(Off)* Good morning sir! *(enter Jenkins and Swotfond.*

Swotfond. Hang we're late!

Jenkins. Of course.

Swotfond. Why "of course"?

Jenkins. Because it's Monday.

Swotfond. What difference does that make?

Jenkins. Why it gives one some time to do the Scripture.

Swotfond. You are a slacker.

Jenkins. I say some one's bagged my book, chuck us yours.

Swotfond. Dashed if I do.

Jenkins. Buck up you fool, progress [emended, in pen, to prayers] is practically over.

Swotfond. You will get into a row with old Gilford.

Jenkins. Buck up man!

Swotfond. Gilford hates slackers.

Jenkins. You are a rotter, they've just finished. *(enter everyone)* Where are we?

Catt. In here.

Jenkins. Why aren't we in Gilford's class room?

Catt. He's ill and isn't coming down to-day, we're with West.

Jenkins.   Bucks, I s'pose it'll be Latin.

(Enter Mr. West, all sit down.)

Mr. West.   Get out your Latin Grammar. I'll give you a few minutes to learn it in.

Swotfond.   Please aren't you going to hear the Scripture?

Mr. West.   No, I'm not.

Swotfond.   But, Sir—

Mr. West.   Did you hear what I said?

Swotfond.   *(Half to himself)* I call it jolly unfair.

Mr. West.   I beg your pardon, what did you say?

Swotfond.   I just said something, sir.

Mr. West.   Get up on that form.

(Enter Mr. Greenfield with visitor.)

Mr. Greenfield.   All right—Carry on you gentlemen. *(Seeing Swotfond)* Hulloa, young man, what are you doing up there?

Mr. West.   He was impertinent, Sir.

Mr. Greenfield.   Any more of that, send him straight to me.

Mr. West.   Yes sir.

(Exit Mr. Greenfield and visitor.)

Mr. West.   Now Catt, kindly tell us "Did[o] driven wild by her horrible designs."

Curtain

Moral.   To do one's prep is merely foolish.
To swank as having done so is criminal.

Volume I, No. 5 September 1916

13   *Things We'd Like to Know*

Did the sudden revival of recruiting in the Heath Mount patrol have anything to do with the Saturday cricket compulsory rule?

Do you like me?

E. W.

14   *Poets' Corner, or, Our Doggerel Depot*

Slipper met a boy
Boy met slipper
Boy didn't mind
Slipper kind
The boy was cheerful
Now he's tearful.

E. W.

[A dozen copies were printed, one specially bound for Arthur
Waugh's birthday, which fell on August 24. For Waugh's comments on the poem, see *A Little Learning*, p. 93. For a description of the book, see G. T. Sims, *The Fiftieth Catalogue* (Hurst,
Reading, Berks.), item 90. Text: *The World to Come: A Poem in
Three Cantos* (privately printed, August 24, 1916), the copy now
in the Humanities Research Center.]

A Poem
In Three Cantos

χὰι εἶδον οὐρανὸν χὰι γῆν χαιὴν.
[And I saw a new heaven and a new earth.]
Rev. xxi.1

August 24th
1916

Canto I

Into Thy hands, o Lord.

The Priest's voice faded in the distance,
Faded till I scarce could hear it,
Till it sounded like the babbling
Of a stream, far distant, running
Through high rocky banks that made it
Echo in a strange contortion
Over space interminable,
Whispering comfort to my dying,
To my pain-racked, weakened senses.
Then it seemed that other faces
Loomed around my gloomy bedside,

Faces that were sad and tear-stained,
Faces that were once familiar,
Yet I could not then remember,
For they seemed to be contorted
By a mist that drew in closer
To my bed, and enveloped
In its clinging waves I struggled,
But I knew that it was useless.
Slowly was I over-powered
And I felt that I was falling
Downwards, downwards, ever downwards,
In the black and gloomy darkness.
Phantoms brushed me, spirits touched me,
Shapes and figures moaning, shrieking,
Past me with a howling shudder,
Left me falling downwards, downwards.
Red mists floated all about me,
Something snapped inside my body,
All was blankness, all was nothing,
Everything was utter blankness. . . .

Great relief came rushing o'er me
Sweeping everything before it,
For I had left pain behind me,
Left it in that great red ocean
Which was seething far behind me.
Then I felt that I was moving,
Moving with a wondrous swiftness,
Like the swallow swooping upward
In the perfect joy of living,
In the joy of nature, sunshine,
And the love of all creation.
Strains of music floated clearly,
Freshening my whole existence,
Like the rain of parchèd flowers.
Music played with skill so wondrous
That it gripped my every tissue,
Brought a joy profound and perfect
To my earth-worn tired spirit.
Then I felt that I was lifted
By a pair of arms so gentle
That, till then, I had not felt them,

Lifted up, and ever upwards
By an angel kind and loving.
Then we seemed to be descending,
And I found we had alighted
On a long and marble terrace
With a flight of steps at one end
Leading to a marble doorway
Covered with a jewelled curtain.
In majesty before the curtain
Stood the great Archangel Michael,
In his hand he held a drawn sword,
A sword that gleamed with wondrous fire,
Fire which was not reflected
But which issued from that keen edge.
Then the great Archangel Michael
Turned to me, and with clear accents
He announced me Heaven's judgment:
"Though thou hast kept God's Commandments
And obeyed His Church's teaching,
Still as thou wast born of woman,
Thou wast born in sin, and even
Though that sin was cleansed in Baptism
Still as thou wast once a sinner,
Thou art ign'rant of the glory
And the majesty of Heaven.
Thou must make the wondrous journey
Through the Kingdom of the Heavens.
Thou must see how man was modelled,
See how prayers ascend to Heaven,
See the torture of the wicked.
Then thou mayest see thy Saviour,
See the God once man incarnate,
Not the humble Jewish peasant
But the Ruler of the Heavens,
At whose word the worlds are shattered,
Tyrants humbled, Poor exalted,
All creation humbly bowing,
Singing, 'Holy, Holy, Holy.'
Then thou mayest see the Father,
He who was before Creation,
At whose word the Heavens were formed,
He who reigned when all was darkness,

Long before the stars were lighted,
When the sun was but a mist cloud
Whirling round and round in darkness,
Making stars and worlds and planets.
Thou mayest see the Holy Spirit,
Gift divine of Christ ascended,
Who conceived the Word incarnate,
Who from Jesus and the Father,
Did'st proceed, and Who descended
On the Holy Church at Whitsun,
Who descends at Confirmation
Who with sevenfold gifts descendeth,
At the Ordination Service.
He whose seven lamps are burning,
He who gives the Absolution
On the poor repenting sinner.
But before thou canst see these things,
Thou must first make the great journey,
Led by Cyprian, the angel,
Who will show you all the wonders,
And explain them, so thou mayest
Understand the infinite glory.
Now go forth—Receive God's blessing,
Return again thou hast seen all,
And art worthy of God's presence."

Canto II

De Profundis

Cyprian led me up a mountain,
Up a steep and rugged mountain,
Till we reached its rocky summit.
"Look," said Cyprian, "On the visions
That I am about to show you.
Thou shalt see prayers unaccepted,
And I will tell you the reason
Why the prayers do not find favour
In the sight of God Almighty.
Look you how the vision formeth,
Shapes itself in uncouth phantom
Slowly growing clearer, clearer,
See the picture slowly painted
Till like this one it is perfect.

Evelyn Waugh, Apprentice

Look, I will explain it later."
I looked down and saw this vision:
A blood-red sun was slowly setting,
Sending forth its scarlet sunbeams,
Dyeing with its crimson tincture
A quiet little country village.
Then like thunder broke resounding
A great cannonade of firing.
Women, children, rushed affrighted
From the fields with cries of horror.
Then the shells came bursting on them,
And in mad confusèd panic,
Shrieking, screaming, rushing, tearing,
They were mown down by the shrapnel.
Then from either side rushed soldiers,
Shouting, shooting, charging, killing,
Up the little cobbled alleys.
Then one party seized the churchyard,
And entrenched behind the grave stones,
Grimly set to work to slaughter.
Then with shouts and screams of anguish
Came charge from right behind them,
And they broke and fled in panic.
In the church the remnants gathered,
Fixed their bayonets, held the doorway,
Till their faces black with powder,
They retreated to the Chancel,
Seized the Cross from off the Altar,
Hurled it 'mongst the approaching number,
Brained with candlesticks the soldiers
Who attempted to attack them.
Then machine guns belched for slaughter,
And they fell choking and shrieking,
Coughing, gasping, and blaspheming,
Soaking with their blood the Sanctuary.
Then the sun set, all was darkness,
And where once Masses were chanted,
Groanings were echoing in the darkness.
As dust came, the vision faded.
Then as I shrank back in horror,
Cyprian bade me go on looking:
And I saw the gleam of candles,

Growing clearer, ever clearer.
And I saw seven lamps a-burning,
Burning red before the Altar.
And I saw before the Altar
Priests and Servers thanking Heaven,
Thanking with their hearts and bodies
For the Victory of their Army,
Thanking for the tortured soldiers,
Thanking for the murdered peasants,
Thanking for their soldiers' outrage
Of the little Oratory.
Thanking that they hurled Madonnas,
Killed with crosses, fought with candles,
Thanking for another anguish,
For 'twas thus their Army conquered.
Then the vision slowly faded,
And another one appearèd;
'Twas the vision of a homestead.
Now bereft of any gladness,
Left alone in abject sorrow
Sat a wretched woman weeping.
On her lap there lay a baby,
A baby that was strangely quiet,
Did not stir, or breathe, or mutter,
For that baby was not living.
In her hand she held a paper
Open at the list of slaughtered,
Then the scene grew dark as midnight,
Swam away and there was nothing.
"That," said Cyprian, "was the Blessing
For which they were thanking Heaven.
This is how mankind interpret
Christ's command to love their foes."
Then appeared another vision,
Being different from the first one,
Not of blood and shrieks of anguish
But of prayers that are accepted.
Cyprian bade me look, and looking
I beheld an Eastern village,
And the steps before the Temple
Crowded with the poor and crippled.
From the Temple came a Moslem

With a kind and gentle bearing.
When he saw the helpless cripples
His whole mind was touched with pity
That he led them to his dwelling,
Set before them all his money,
All his food, and all his clothing,
Gave them food, lodging and shelter,
And prayed for them morning and night.
Then the scene before us melted,
And his prayers echoed in heaven.

Canto III

Mea Maxima Culpa

Cyprian bore me a plateau,
To a cold and wind-swept plateau
Swept by tempests howling round us
Whistling, screaming as they past us
On their way to sweep the heavens.
In the centre loomed a tower,
Gloomy, dark, grim and forbidding.
On its portals hung a parchment,
Hung a yellow, musty, parchment,
On which was inscribed in letters
Of the blackest ever written:
"Weeping shall there be in plenty,
Crime and wickedness and torture,
For this is the home of Satan,
Here the serpent which made Adam
Drink the juice of fruit forbidden
To his own eternal torture
Lives until the day of judgment.
Here the Devil laid his wager,
And on Job did cast derision.
Hence the cruelties of Nero,
Hence the anguish of the Martyrs,
Hence the wailing of the slaughtered
And the shrieking of the murdered.
Here was hatched our Lord's betrayal,
Here the thirty silver pieces,
Here Christ's Church was first divided
In this home of crime and torture."
Cyprian approached the entrance,

Traced Christ's Cross upon the portals,
And they, shivering, fell inwards
As if moved by an eruption.
Up a dank and moss-grown staircase
Crusted with the filth of ages
We ascended in the darkness,
Through the foul air we ascended
Upwards, upwards, ever upwards,
Till we'd climbed the topmost turret.
Then he drew me on a platform,
On a high and shiv'ring platform
Far above the gloomy plateau,
High above all earthly buildings,
Looming over space gigantic,
Overshadowing all the Heavens,
Gaunt and black against the sky-line.
All about us roared a tempest,
Round us lightning flashed in fury,
And the winds in fierce defiance
Threatened to hurl us downwards,
Where the thunder roaring loudly
Mingled in most ghastly music
With the wailing of the tortured.
Then the wind grew still more angry,
And the stones began to crumble
As all space arose to meet us,
Shrieking, whistling, howling past us,
Whirling in impotent fury.
Cyprian held a Cross above him,
And the elements in frenzy
Dashed themselves to utter silence
On the turrets of their prison.
Then amid the sudden silence
There rang out a blast of trumpets,
Ringing in discordant echoes,
Through the utter void around us
Till it rang itself to silence.
At the sound of that fell music
All creation seemed to quiver,
And the turret shook with terror
Worse than in the tempests' fury.
Then there floated by in grandeur,

Evelyn Waugh, Apprentice

Rank on rank of Satan's courtiers,
Beasts, that baffle all description,
Mingled half and half with humans,
Creatures with the hearts of devils,
Beauty, cruelty and madness
Mingled with deceit most vile,
Howling round our quivering platform.
Then appeared a long procession,
Bearing flaring blood-red torches.
Then there came a dreadful silence.
Suddenly in crime majestic,
Throned in carnage, shrined in bloodshed,
Came the prince of all most evil.
He, once angel, now thrice devil,
Swept before us in derision.
As he past he turned round saying
In a voice that chilled all Heaven:
"Coward, cursed, I spit upon thee.
Thou did'st fear the burning fires,
So thou bowed before the Altar,
Like the terror-stricken Angels
Whimp'ring, 'Holy, Holy, Holy,'
In the hope of being saved.
And the ones that had the courage
To rebel against the Tyrant
Thou did'st shrink from in abhorrence,
In self-righteous terror cringing
Lest thou mightest be defiled,
Thou who art more cursed than any."
And he swept away in laughter,
Laughing to his own damnation.

As I stood before the entrance
'Bout to enter Heaven's Glory,
Cyprian bade me farewell, saying
In a voice most sweet and tender:
"Now my pleasant task is ended,
We have travelled far together
And have viewed all heaven's glory,
But the time is now approaching
When we pass on different missions,
I to pilot wandering spirits,

You to go before your Maker.
Now farewell, your time approaches,"
And I turned towards the entrance.

Finis

Part Two The Lancing Years

Valentine
To Mr. Bottomly

[The manuscript is undated, but it has been torn from the same notebook as "To a Dilettante" (B6), copied in Waugh's diary entry for August 10, 1920 (*Diaries,* p. 95). Nothing in the checkered careers of Horatio Bottomley can be used to date this more specifically. Bottomley was the jingo editor of *John Bull,* member of Parliament, convicted in 1922 of embezzling war funds. (See A. J. P. Taylor, *English History 1914-1945* (New York and Oxford: Oxford University Press, 1965), p. 21n. and passim.) Text: Manuscript in the Humanities Research Center, *Catalogue,* B4.]

There are more things in earth and heaven above —
(You don't count heaven, Horatio? — as you please —)
— than you ere dream of. Not the least of these,
As someone said — not in John Bull is Love.

17   *Convention*

["Convention" is dated October 3, 1920; "Maps," which follows, October 10. Waugh had returned to Lancing on September 17 and was already ragging the Officer Training Corps (*Diaries*, pp. 104–106). "Convention" was perhaps based on a more general mood. Text: Manuscript in the Humanities Research Center, *Catalogue*, C2.]

When Mr. Bernard Shaw comes to a first night in grey woolen shirt, brown homespuns and brogue shoes, the people in the stalls are thoroughly amused. To the suburbans in the dress circle he comes as a personal affront.

When a woman has to entertain, with no natural charm or tact, she is forced to use a code of etiquette and manners which a good hostess would observe or disregard unconsciously and with equal success.

When a doctor has bought a practice, he is at liberty to torment and kill his patients, as he sees fit, without interruption from rivals or patients, for only thus are the incompetent able to earn a living.

Convention is the self protection of the mediocrities; and it is for just this reason that it is most important for cleverer people to respect the shams they can so easily despise. Mr. Bernard Shaw acts as a cad in offending those earnest middle classes who have paid eight and sixpence for their seats.

The mystic knows that he is nearer God on the downs than in a Baptist Chapel, but it would be just as much a crime against his religion to disturb a service there as to participate in one.

The fundamental cynicism of life is clothed by the mediocrities; if anyone can see its true nakedness, the least they can do is courteously to look away.

18 *Maps*

To motorists and militarists is given a special genius for ruining beautiful things; it is to these that maps make the greatest appeal.

To the motorist a map is only as a list of wedding presents is to a burglar. It opens for him fresh vistas of smoke and dust and reechoes with the prospects of new hoots and explosions.

To the militarist it means far more; it is an epitome of all that he holds most holy and most great. It is in it's lust for maps that the full subtlety of the bellicose mind is revealed.

To see a beautiful stretch of country shrivelled up, flattened out, discoloured and laboriously subdivided; to see high hills and valleys reduced to pink circles; to see nineteenth century pseudo-Gothic and early Saxon Churches degraded to the same "conventional sign," are the ideals for which soldiers are willing to live and die; these are the ideals for which they will keep awake in military school.

19

Fragment of a Novel

[According to the *Diaries,* Waugh conceived the idea for the novel in late October, 1920, just after a visit from his brother, Alec. He worked on the manuscript until late December and had abandoned it by January 10, 1921. See *Diaries,* pp. 107, 108. The marginal notes in pencil, given in brackets, were probably made by Arthur Waugh or, with less likelihood, by Alec Waugh.

Mr. Boyle's history lecture is cribbed almost directly, as Waugh indicates, from Sir Richard Lodge's *The Students Modern Europe: A History of Modern Europe, from the Capture of Constantinople by the Turks to the Treaty of Berlin, 1878,* chapter 15, sections 8 and 9. The Lecky whom he recommends for Catherine the Great is William Edward Hartpole Lecky; the book is probably *History of England in the XVIII Century,* chapter 19. Text: Manuscript in the Humanities Research Center, *Catalogue,* A6.]

To myself,

Evelyn Arthur St. John Waugh

to whose sympathy and appreciation alone it owes its being,
this book is dedicated.

Dedicatory letter,

My dear Evelyn,

Much has been written and spoken about the lot of the boy with literary aspirations in a philistine family; little can adequately convey his difficulties, when the surroundings, which he has known from childhood, have been entirely literary. It is a sign of victory over these difficulties that this book is chiefly, if at all, worthy of attention.

Many of your relatives and most of your father's friends are more or less directly interested in paper and print. Ever since you first left the nursery for meals with your parents downstairs, the conversation, to which you were an insatiable listener, has been of books, their writers and producers; ever since, as a sleepy but triumphantly emancipate school-boy, you were allowed to sit up with our elders in the "bookroom" after dinner, you have heard little but discussion about books. Your home has always been full of them; all new books of any merit, and most of none, seem by one way or another to find their place in the files which have long overflowed the shelves. Among books your whole life has been layed and you are now rising up in your turn to add one more to the everlasting bonfire of the ephemeral.

And all this will be brought up against you. "Another of these precocious Waughs," they will say, "one more nursery novel." So be it. There is always a certain romance, to the author at least, about a first novel which no reviewer can quite shatter. Good luck! You have still high hopes and big ambitions and have not yet been crushed in the mill of professionalism. Soon perhaps you will join the "word-smiths" jostling one another for royalties and contracts, meanwhile you are still very young.

Yourself,
Evelyn

Chapter one.

Peter Audley awoke with "second bell" ringing dismally down the cloisters and rolling over in bed looked at his watch. Reassured that he had another five minutes before he need begin getting up, he pulled his rug up over his shoulders and lay back gazing contentedly down the dormitory, which was already stirring with the profoundly comforting sounds made by other people dressing. The splashing of the showers next door, the chipping of the thick crockery and the muttered oaths at backstuds accentuated the pleasure of the last minutes.

Early school was kept up practically all the year round at Selchurch, which took a certain pride in [the] gloom of these early mornings. Peter, however, had got his "privileges" which took away the bitterest sting of frantic punctuality and allowed him, after reporting to his form master, to sit out and work in his study.

Evelyn Waugh, Apprentice

With a heave he got out of bed and went to wash. The showers looked singularly uninviting but the water for the basins was stone cold — the furnaces were not lit until midday in March 1918 — and with rising gloom he returned shivering and half dry to the dormitory. Some fanatic had opened one of the high Gothic windows and a cold gust of wind swept down the room. There was a chorus of protestation and the window was closed. He dressed dully [?] and leaving the dormitory at a few minutes past seven crossed the quad to "report." Several fags, laden with books, dashed past him, trying desperately to avoid recognition by the prefect "taking lates." His form master nodded to him and he turned on his heel and made for his study. The gravel was dark with fallen rain, the sky menacing with monstrous rough hewn clouds; over everything spread a fine, wet mist. [Pencil note: "avoid inversion."]

The handle of his study door was cold; he went in, kicked the door to and fell into an easy chair gazing round the tiny room. It was pleasant enough and he had spent considerable pains on it, but this morning it afforded him no pleasure.

The carpet was black — a burst of aestheticism which he had long regretted as it took a great deal of brushing and earned his study the name of the "coal cellar" — and the walls distempered a bluish grey. [Pencil note: New sentence (?): The walls were] On them were hung four large Medici prints, the gift of his grandmother but his own choice; Botticelli's Mars & Venus — he had had some difficulty over this with his house master, to whom a nude was indecent whether it came from the National Gallery or La Vie Parisienne — Beatrice d'Este, Rembrandt's "Philosopher" and Holbein's Duchess of Milan. These he liked either because they were very beautiful or because they gave an air of distinction which his friends' Harrison Fishers and Rilette pictures lacked. [Pencil note: "'both and' This sentence means nothing. *You* know whether he liked. The author is *omniscient*."] The curtains, cushions on the window seat and table cloth were blue; the whole room was pleasantly redolent of the coffee of the evening before.

Peter, however, lay back staring gloomily at the grey block of class rooms opposite. It was Saturday morning and Saturday afternoon was the time chosen, as being the longest uninterrupted time in the week, for the uniform parade. He could just remember when, his first term, summer 1914, it had been the great social time of the week when tea was brewed and quantities of eclaires eaten, and now that he had grown to an age to have a study and enjoy these things, they were all blotted out and from two to six he would have to manoeuvre a section of sullen fags over the wet downs in some futile "attack scheme." [Pencil note: "avoid long sentences."]

He knew exactly what would happen. They would fall in on one of the quads and be inspected — that meant half an hours work with reeking brasso and s.a.p. cleaning his uniform and equipment. They would then march up to the downs and in a driving wind stand easy while the O.C. explained the afternoons work. Ordnance maps would be issued to all N.C.O.s with which to follow the explanation; these always bulged with incorrect folding and flapped in the wind.

It was never considered sufficient for one company merely to come and attack the other; a huge campaign of which they formed a tiny part would have to be elaborated. A company would be the advanced guard of part of an army, which had landed at Littlehampton and was advancing upon Hasting, intending to capture important bridge heads on the local river on their way; B company, with white hat bands, would be a force set to hold the spur of the downs above the Sanatorium cooperating with hypothetical divisions on either flank, until another division could arrive from Arundel. Rattles would be issued to serve as Lewis guns and this game of make-believe would go on for three hours, with extreme discomfort to both sides, when whistles and bugles would sound and the corps form up again for a criticism of the afternoon's work. They would be told that, when the parade was dismissed, all rifles were to be wiped over with an oily rag before being returned to the armoury and that all uniforms were to be back in the lockers before six o'clock. They would then dismiss, hungry, bad tempered and with only twenty minutes in which to change for Chapel.

He hated the corps and all the more now that he had to take it seriously. He was seventeen and a half; next year, if the war was still on, as it showed every sign of being, would see him fighting. It brought everything terribly near. He had learnt much of what it was like over there from his brother, but Ralf saw everything so abstractedly with such imperturbable cynicism. Peter flattered himself that he was far more sensitive and temperamental. He was sure that he would not be able to stand it; Ralf had won the D.S.O. some months ago.

He collected his thoughts with a start and looked at his time table. He had to finish the chapter of Economics which he had left the evening before. The book was lying where he had tossed it and, like everything that morning, looked singularly uninviting. It was bound in a sort of greasy, limp, oil cloth, "owing," a label half scraped off the back proclaimed, "to shortage of labour"; it was printed crookedly on a thin greyish paper with little brown splinters of wood in it; it was altogether a typical piece of wartime workmanship. He took it up with listless repulsion and began to read.

"From considerations of this nature," he read, "which, while not true of every person, taken individually, are yet on the average true, it may be inferred, with approximate accuracy, that by adding to the wealth of the poor, something taken, by some recognised and legal process, from the wealth of the rich, while some dissatisfaction as well as satisfaction is inevitably caused, yet, provided that the poor be greater in number than the rich, the satisfaction is greater than the dissatisfaction. Inequality of wealth, insofar as. . ." [Pencil note in form of large, vague question mark.]

It was all ineffably tedious. He tossed the book on to the table in the corner and taking up a novel passed the next half hour in dissatisfied gloom.

2

The clock in the quad struck quarter to eight and voices and shuffling sounded across the gravel as the forms began emptying. The door of his study was burst open and Bellinger came in.

"Edifying spectacle of history specialist at work! Here have I been doing geography with the 'door mouse' for three mortal quarters of an hour, while you read low novels."

Bellinger was in the army class, a cheery soul, athletic, vacant, with an obsession for clothes. This was the only subject about which he could talk [pencil insert: "with authority"; may be EW's]; he was always perfectly dressed himself and had earned something of a reputation by it. People would bring him patterns of cloth and consult him when they were getting suits, which was complimentary, although they never took his advice. It was said of him that he had once cut the headmaster in London because he met him wearing a brown overcoat with evening dress.

Peter turned down the corner of his page—a pernicious habit even in a wartime "Outlines of Economics" of which he could never cure himself—and got up.

"Come across to hall, you silly old ass, and tell me the latest bulletins from Sackville Street."

"Nothing doing," said Bellinger with the self righteous gloom of one whose religion has been insulted and pulled at the points of his waistcoat, "nothing doing at all. It's the curse of this infernal war. While all the best people are in uniform they don't pay any attention to civilian fashions. Thank the Lord I shall be in khaki in a couple of months."

They linked up and walked down to hall, Bellinger earnestly enlarging upon the advantages of the R.A.F. over the ordinary uniform.

When they arrived at the "pits-table," where people with studies sat, a heated discussion was going on. The head, Peter gathered, had proposed to the Games Committee the night before that none of the house cups should be competed for until after the war and that the time saved should be devoted to more parades and longer digging upon the house potatoe plots. Cook, the captain of Lane's, had apparently been the only one with the courage to hold out against him. Lane's were certain to get the open football and stood a good chance for the Five Mile.

Beaton, a small science specialist, was voluble in the head's defence.

"After all," he was saying, "what effects has the war had on us here? We've had a little less food and coal, people have been leaving a little earlier, the young masters have gone and these antiquated old fools like Boyle have taken their places, parades have become a bit longer, but is this enough? Has anything been done to make us realise that we are in the middle of the biggest war in history?"

"Everything has been done," said Peter, "to make school life excessively unpleasant — after you with the bread, please Travers — what little of the old life does remain, is what keeps it just tolerable. [Pencil note: "Clumsy."] Good God, isn't it bad enough for you. I pity the men who've come during the last year and know only this side of Selchurch. I hate school, now, and shall be only too glad to get away; why utterly spoil it for the 'underschools'?"

"Yes," said Travers a large, sad "historian" on the other side of the table, "You seem to be one of the maniacs who believe in making themselves wretched because other people are. It's only by the misery of three quarters, that life can be even tolerable for a quarter of society. It's unjust but it's better than the whole show being miserable. It's a fundamental principle of political science" — any particularly sweeping cynicism was a "fundamental principle" with Travers.

"My pater had that craze badly in 1914," said Garth, a pleasant, spotty youth, next to Peter, "he dug up the tennis court to grow vegetables when there was plenty of waste ground behind the stable yard."

Evelyn Waugh, Apprentice

"And the mater makes me wear old clothes," said Bellinger, "because she thinks it looks bad to wear new ones in war time."

"Everyone is quite imbecile about the war" — Travers loved dismissing subjects — "they don't realise that it is a natural function of development. It's a fundamental principle that society can only remain normal if it is decimated at regular periods."

The "paper boy" came to the table. Every day it was the duty of one of the fags to fetch the house papers from the porter's lodge, as soon as he came out of early school, and bring them up to hall. They were supposed to go to the people who had bought them at the "paper auction" at the beginning of term, but in practice they went first to the high table where the prefects sat with the housemaster; when they had made their choice, he took them to the "pits-table" and distributed what were left as he liked.

"Times, please" said Peter over his shoulder.

"I'm sorry, Audley, that's gone."

"All right, Morning Post. Thanks."

He spread it out over the table and glanced down the columns. It was full of the usual war news (Peter wondered vaguely what they managed to put in the papers in peace time); there were rumours of preparations for a big German offensive, factious political questions in the house, pages of minor engagements in the East. He folded it and passed it on to Bellinger.

3

It was a gloomy morning; gloomy even for the Easter term 1918. For half an hour after breakfast he sat in his study cleaning his uniform; in chapel he could smell the cleaning stuff up his nails. [Pencil mark like large *F* in margin.] After chapel he had to go in for a double period of European History. He went into school profoundly depressed.

The "historians" were now taken by one Boyle. He had been, until the outbreak of war, the headmaster of a prosperous preparitory school on the East coast and had lived a life of lucrative dignity, making himself agreeable to distinguished parents and employing a large and competent staff to do the teaching. For two years he had kept doggedly on, feeling that it would be a surrender to the barbarian enemy if he left, but the numbers steadily sank, until one night a bomb was actually dropped onto the gymnasium breaking every frame of glass in the house. Then he realised that he must give it up, "St. Pendred's" was commandeered to house a garrison staff, and Mr. Boyle set about finding other employment.

The head forced to choose between Mr. Boyle and a mistress, to his eternal discredit chose Mr. Boyle and in less than a year the Senior History Specialist Set had sunk from the intellectual mekka of the school to the haven which sheltered those who considered that the work they had had to do to pass the School Certificate absolved them from any further exertions, at any rate, while they were at Selchurch. Not that he was ragged — that would have been beneath the dignity of a Sixth Form set — They merely sat through his hours in complete apathy. His predecessor had been a young man fresh from Cambridge and had made his history extremely entertaining, they had held debates, read each other papers and discussed current politics, but now there were no Varsity scholarships, the battle clouds of France shut out all but the immediate future and no one had any particular motive for, or interest in, working. Mr. Boyle certainly had not and Youth, far from being the time of burning quests and wild, gloriously vain ideals beloved of the minor poets, is essentially one of languor and repose. Every hour he dictated notes, from a large leather bound note book, which most people took; every week he set an essay which several people wrote; every month he gave out a syllabus of books for out of school study, which nobody read. He asked for little and was content with far less but the Senior History Specialist set often seemed unsatisfactory even to Mr. Boyle.

He came into the class room smiling a dignified welcome all round, laid his note book on one side of the high oak desk, his mortar board on the other, and sat down smoothing out his gown.

"Good morning, gentlemen," he began in his usual formula, "What are we doing this morning? European history, isn't it Travers? Thank you. Ah yes, well I don't think we can do better than go on with our notes for a little. Now let me see where was it we had got to. Alberoni? Yes I see I have the place marked. The last thing I gave you was 'willing to cede Sardinia to secure her nephew's succession to the Duchy of Parma' wasn't it? Well then, head this 'D. Alberoni's third coalition.'" For two [hours he dictated an essay on XVIIth [actually XVIII] diplomacy.

Peter had reduced the talking of notes to an entirely subconscious exercise. He could now sit schooled by long practice, with his mind completely blank or filled with other things while his pen wrote out pages of notes industriously and quite correctly. Sometimes he would be woken from his reverie by a pause over some proper name, but often on looking them through he would find names which he had no recollection of having heard before. He sat writing out,

"... invited 'pretender' to Spain and arranged with Görz a northern alliance with Sweden and Russia to support the Stuart claims, while at the same time he entered into correspondence with Polignac and the Duchess of Main, to overthrow the Regency. The death of Charles XII, however...."

Mr. Boyle's notes did not elucidate any difficult problems or sift the important facts of history from the trivial. They merely stated things in direct paraphrase of Lodge; for the whole double period Peter steadily took them down.

At last the clock chimed and Mr. Boyle stood up, shut his note book and took up his mortar board. "That will be enough for this morning, I think. Remember that I want the essays on 'The Freedom of the civilized State' by Monday evening, without fail this time please. I will ask you to read up Catherine the Great for next Tuesday, if you will—I recommend Lecky. Thank you, good morning."

Wearily they filed out for break. In the war time efficiency mania P.T. had been innovated which effectually took up all the break—ten minutes in which to change and twenty minutes drill. Peter hurried to the changing room and began undressing; he suddenly remembered that he had broken the lace of his gym shoe the day before. He succeeded in borrowing another and then realised that he had forgotten to get a new hat for parade as he had been told to last time. Everything seemed to be conspiring against him this morning.

"You never lose a stud but you lose the lot," sighed Bellinger, "Hullo, what the devil does *he* want."

Peter looked round and saw the porter's burly figure framed in the doorway.

"Telegram for Mr. Audley, sir."

"Hullo, what?" Peter tore open the orange envelope and hurriedly took out the telegram; it was getting late for P.T.

"Ralf on leave," it ran, "return home wiring head will meet 4:52 Bulfrey."

4

One of the awfully clever things that Ralf had said was that life should be divided into water tight compartments and that no group of friends or manner of living should be allowed to encroach upon any other. Peter lay back and compared the day with the prospects early that morning.

As soon as he had got the telegram he had put on his shoes and told the porter to 'phone for a taxi. After a frantic search for his house master and an incoherent but convincing explanation to him and a hurried interview with the matron about his bag, he had managed to get away in time to catch the 11:12 to Victoria. There he had had a hasty but excellent lunch at the Grosvenor and had dashed across to Paddington and got into the train just as it was starting.

He now had a clear two hours run to Bulfrey. He lay back and took a cigarette from the box he had bought at lunch. Very contentedly he watched the telegraph wires rising falling and recrossing each other, mile after mile.

He had not had time in the rush of half packed pyjamas, moving trains and lost tickets, to think of what it all meant; now in the empty first class carriage with magazines and cigarettes he began to shake off the shadows of [the] prison house. He looked at his watch. At the very time that he was swaying into the country through the short wayside stations, Bellinger and Beaton and Garth and everyone else with whose lives his own had seemed so inextricably bound that morning were marching about on the downs. It was very cold at Selchurch, he reflected and the sea mist was lying in the valleys; he was warm with the close atmosphere of the carriage and the glass of port he had had after lunch and with a deep inward content.

Mile succeeded mile through the avenue of telegraph poles. Outside the weather was clearing up and a bright cool sun came out. He watched the fields reeling by and began to pass the landmarks which had grown familiar through many home coming, an imposing patent medicine factory, the neat beds of a large market garden, an Elizabethan farmhouse.

He wondered how long this unexpected holiday was going to last; he supposed about four days. This was really the first time that Ralf had made any mark in his [pencil insert: "Peter's"] life; he was five years older and had always kept himself very much aloof. They had had many quarrels as brothers always have. At time[s] Ralf had been almost a prig, particularly when he was head of the house at Selchurch, and [pencil insert: "during"] his first year at Oxford. Anyway it was through him that Peter was now sitting in comfort instead of marching his section up a wet hill in "blob" formation, and in the warmth of heart that can come only from physical comfort, Peter prepared to be very gracious towards his brother.

At last the train slowed to a stop and stood panting but unexhausted like a well trained runner. [Pencil: "good."] Peter suddenly realised that they had reached Bulfrey. He snatched up his hat and bag, buttoned his coat and leapt onto the platform. Ralf was striding down towards him.

Peter had seen him in uniform before but then it had been with the timid pride of a 1914 subaltern. Now after three years fighting he looked wonderfully fit and hansome. A slanting ray of sunlight lit up his fair hair; he was wearing no cap.

"Hullo, Peter," he cried, shaking hands, "we were afraid that you mightn't be able to get the train. I suppose you've had lunch?"

"Yes thanks, I managed to get some in town. Pretty fair rush though. Hold on a second while I find my ticket." He handed Ralf his bag and began exploring his pockets. Finding it, at last, between the leaves of his school "blue-book," he gave it to the collector and taking back his bag followed his brother out.

"Is that all the luggage you've got?" he asked, "That's splendid; we shall be able to bring it up with us now. I've got the dog-cart outside. Moira's looking after it. She was coming into Bulfrey to do some shopping so I asked her to come and meet you."

Moira Gage was the daughter of the vicar of Bulfrey Combe. Peter's age, she and her brother had been the constant companions of the Audley boys before they went to school. They had seen less of each other as they grew up, Chris had gone to Winchester, Ralf and Peter to Selchurch, but the Vicarage was next door to the Hall and they had seen a good deal of each other in the holidays. Their fathers were close friends.

"Good work, I was afraid she would be away doing that V.A.D. work. I only saw her once all last holidays. Ah there she is."

They had come out into the small station yard. On the other side of it stood the dog-cart and in it stood Moira Gage, one hand holding the reins, the other shading her eyes. She was tall, slim and pale, not really pretty but graceful and attractive; from a distance she looked like a Shepperson drawing [pencil: "Clumsy"; underlining of Shepperson] but when you got nearer you saw depths in her grey, scrutable eyes, which his charming mannerisms could never convey; she was dressed in a tweed coat and a skirt with a grey silk scarf over her shoulders. Peter ran forward and greeted her.

"Peter," she said, "before you do anything else, do make Ralf put his hat on. He looks simply dreadful and I'm sure he'd be court-martialled or something, if anyone saw."

"Three years of military life shatter any illusions about military discipline," Ralf replied, climbing up into the dog cart, "the only hardened militarist nowadays is the newly conscripted civilian."

"Now he's being clever again," Moira laughed, "I really thought you lost that when you came down from Oxford. Among other things, it's very bad manners when you are in stupid company."

"Thank you," Peter expostulated, "I wish you'd speak for yourself. I'm in the sixth now and write essays on industrial history and all sorts of things."

"You seem to regard you[r] history with most unreasonable pride," said Moira, "from all I hear it sounds only slack."

"All pride is unreasonable" said Ralf. To Peter it seemed that he had paused a moment hesitating whether "no pride is unreasonable" was the more impressive; he had long gone beyond the stage when a sweeping generalisation could pass as an epigram.

"The aphorisms of a disappointed man," said Moira. [Pencil: "She would not anticipate Barbillion."] "The next remark like that Ralf and I get out and walk."

Bulfrey Combe was a mile and a half out from Bulfrey and still kept most of the appearance of a country village. Bulfrey was a small town with two or three streets of cheap shops, a bank, and a small glass factory which formed the nucleus of a large area of slums which was gradually spreading its grimy tentacles along the roads into the [MS ends.]

[According to Waugh's diary entry for February 3, 1921: "In the evening, during evening school, I suddenly thought of the 'mute magnificence of death' and so wrote some verses which I dispatched this morning to *Public School Verse*. The original phrase was lost, as is usual in verbal inspirations, and the whole was very self-conscious — 'mean adventurings' etc. — but I hope that they take it so that I can collect the signed copy I had thought of months ago." The rejection notice reached Waugh on March 1 (*Diaries*, pp. 110, 114). Text: Manuscript in the Humanities Research Center, *Catalogue*, B7.]

Erga vivida vis animie [?] pervicit et extra
processit longe flammantia moenia mundi.[1]

Among the mean adventuring of men,
Godlike he walked and like a man he died;
He passed the taunting mediocrities
Smiling, supreme & unaccompanied.

With all the cold magnificence of death,
He passed into the Darkness where at length
He could stretch out his great and weary limbs
Rejoicing in the long repose of strength.
Or he could find refulgent in the dark
Great kindred spirits long misunderstood
And with them talk through individed days
Of all their ills and find the talking good.

And yet not wholly happily because
So far was he above the frenzied stress

---

[1] "Therefore the living power of the soul will prevail and will proceed far beyond the flaming walls of the universe."

Of all the little men that hated him,
That he could love them for their littleness.

And sometimes, when the prolix Great
had talked for timeless nights in courteous debate
He would look down and long to see a man
Who had a heart and bore a frown of hate.

21

The Twilight of Language

[This is the only known surviving document from the meetings of the Dilettanti, a club for the discussion of politics, literature, and art founded in November, 1919, by Roger Fulford, A. E. H. Molson ("Preters" in the diaries), Dudley Carew, and Waugh. For Waugh's comments on the Dilettanti, see *Diaries,* pp. 34ff., and *A Little Learning,* pp. 128–29. Text: Manuscript in the Humanities Research Center, *Catalogue,* C3.]

For the Dilettanti. Sunday Feb. 13th 1921

Mr. Chairman and Gentlemen,

Anyone who has read much modern literature will have been struck with its abnormality in subject and treatment, an abnormality which is generally unpleasant and, I contend, always inartistic. The object of this paper is to suggest a reason for this and a possible cure.

The reason is, I think[,] that language has become worn out. The cure is a new movement which is only in its infancy and of which I shall speak later.

Language was presumably an advance upon a sort of "deaf and dumb" code. When the first apeman conversed with the second, his needs were so simply the mere animal wants of food and rest, that he could adequately say what he wanted in gestures. If he wanted food he could point to his mouth, if he wanted a fight he could throw a stone. But soon his needs became more elaborate and the calls upon his ingenuity more frequent and it was then that he established a convention of vocal gestures which we call words.

This is, of course, an a priori supposition and probably has not historical foundation but it sounds plausible and shows, what is undoubtedly true, that language is simply a convention and cre-

ation of man. A certain number of men collected together &
decided that a noise "cow" should represent among them their
conception of that animal; as their life became fuller they devised
fresh noises to represent the new things they found and so languages
were formed.

This was both the foundation and decay of literature because it
founded it upon an untenable position. To start with it limited an
author's public inestimably (I use the word public in its true sense. I
do not mean the vulgar idea of the people who will buy a book &
increase the author's income—though of course, since even poets
must eat, this is an implicit consideration—but what I mean is that a
great work of art can only fully be appreciated by a small portion of
the world. Thus it loses what should be one of the essential qualities
of art—it is no longer universal. When a man has painted a great
picture etc. [this clause inserted between lines.] When a man has
written a Great Book perhaps twenty thousand of his countrymen
can enjoy it. No foreigner however well taught can really appreciate
the full subtleties of another language and all translations are of
necessity impoverished, because no two words ever mean the same.
It is doubtful indeed whether one word ever means quite the same
to two people. Certainly if you look up a word in a foreign dictionary
the translation you are given, except of course for a definite noun
like "sugar" or "ink[,]" would not have all the shades of meaning of
the original.

And so we come to the other great point. Words have become too
subtle[;] they have been used so often that their meanings have
become enlarged and confused. They are like painting rags which
have entirely lost their original colours. Every time they are used
they get some slight deviation of meaning. You can see how much
language has changed by reading any early prose and verse. If you
look through any glossary of Shakespeare or Milton you will see the
original meanings of words no[w] used entirely differently.

Some words have not only deviated but come to mean almost
exactly the opposite. As for instance "admire" which has lost its
original meaning of "wonder at." In *Hamlet* when Rosencrantz
wishes to tell Hamlet how disgusted his mother is at his conduct,
he says

"Your behavior hath struck her into amazement and
admiration."

And when Hamlet, earlier in the play, says,
"I'll make a ghost of him that lets me," he means "of him that
prevents me."

Evelyn Waugh, Apprentice

Everyone must have had instances of this shewn him by zealous form masters ad nauseam so I will not emphasize this.

But more than this words have been so coupled and combined as to make one naturally associate one with the other and so as to make them uncompatable. This is a bad sentence—I will try and put it better. What I mean is that certain words have been used together so often that they have become clichés. There are many nouns which have a stock adjective applied to them by all journalists and most lady novelists.

"Faultless evening dress"; "implicit faith"; "effete aristocracy"; "lavish display."

There are hundreds of words inevitably coupled together like this; originally they were appropriate but now they are simply used automatically like inseparable friends who are never spoken of singly. The result of this has been the craving for startling epithets which marks so much modern verse. Great men can do this safely. When Rupert Brooke wrote "When your swift hair is quiet in death," he was not using the adjective simply like a capital letter to attract attention. He was applying an entirely new idea to "hair," you could describe it as "curly" or "red" or "long" or, if you felt more worked up as "iridescent" or "silken" or "wanton" but to describe it as "swift" was what only Rupert Brooke could do. It introduces an entirely new conception of hair and one that is true. You will find if you think about it that "swift" is the perfect adjective for some sorts of hair.

That was all right but soon it got taken up by people of inferior perception and greater ingenuity. We soon got, I think it was Robert Nichols describing,

"Drunkenness streaming in colours"

and Edith Sitwell writing,

"The sunlight coughed, as white as chalk."

which, as the mathematicians say, is absurd.

But more than this one cannot now describe anything simply. It is not enough to say what a thing is, you must say what no one but you ever thought it was. Everything has been said simply and the time has come to find something outrageous and original to say if you want a hearing.

Some of the most magnificent things that have been said in English are perfectly simple. I do not think that any line has been written in English dramatic verse to equal Webster's words over the body of the Duchess of Malfi:

"cover her face; mine eyes dazzle; she died young"

is the most dignified, pathetic and simple line in English verse. But this has been said. A modern reader wants more than dignity, pathos and simplicity. In Genesis God was content to say "It is not good that the man should be alone: I will make an help meet for him."

But when Mr. Arthur Symons wished to express the same sentiments some thousands of years later, he had to say

> "Each in himself his hour to be and cease
>   Endured alone. But who of men would dare
> Sole with himself his single burden bear
> All the long day until the night's release?"

In the same way in prose one cannot tell a simple story. All the essential primitive stories have been written. One man hating another or loving a woman or fighting a great battle or discovering a faery land — all these very excellent stories have been told thousands of times and so the modern novel is generally of two kinds, either a long series of conversations on general topics like Mr. Arnold Lunn's or stories of abnormalities, and these are the more numerous, horrible studies in different forms of crime and lunacy, grotesque and indecent and morbid. I don't think that I have found a novel written during the last five years which has pretensions to being literary, in which there is a single character who is not completely odious and repugnant.

And this sort of novel has entered during the last two years into another phase, in which it assumes such a frantic obscurity of form that it takes an immense amount of intellectual concentration and a great many readings to elucidate any meaning at all. These are mostly written by women. I don't know whether anyone here has read "Bliss" a book of short stories by Catherine [*sic*] Mansfield. I am told that it is incomparably excellent and, I must say, that I liked those that I could understand very much. But many of them are quite unmeaning at a first reading and it takes at least three to grasp the general trend of events at all. For example, to parody her style, an author fifty years ago might have written,

> "It was a cold November night and a heavy wind was beating round the house. Ursula sat over the fire and waited for Jimmy to come, trying the while to read her book."

Catherine Mansfield would write about ten pages straight off like this,

"November—and a great grey wind dashing into everything, stirring up leaves. Copper leaves and a grey wind. Well he'd come tonight—but the wind kept beating about and saying 'Ursula'—but then the wind can't talk. That all a wind is [*sic*]. I like a tag[?] like that, it occurred to me in bed about the wind saying 'Ursula'—even a grey wind. What was the book about. Not about a grey wind and copper leaves anyway but then the wind was so noisy. It had been like that ten years ago—but that was before Jimmie's time and he was coming tonight through the grey wind. Saying 'Ursula' all the time. But then I don't believe in winds or copper leaves—not really copper at least"

and so on. This is honestly not an exaggeration of her style in some of her stories. You can imagine that they take some reading.

[Undated, but probably early 1921. Text: Manuscript in the
Humanities Research Center, *Catalogue,* A8.]

"Oh, yes," said Lurnstein, "I had ideals at one time all right — we all
do, you know."

He was leaning back from the small table, on which the tea was
set, eyeing my half finished portrait. I had had a long sitting and his
beautiful china tea in his thin blue and white china came as a great
relief.

He looked extremely handsome, I thought, in the golden afternoon light, in his picturesque studio overall; Jewish, of course, but
with a distinguished air that made one overlook his stumpy hands
and other signs of ill-breeding.

"Perhaps you'd like to hear something of my life," he said, "it has
not been without interest."

He lit another cigarette, pushed the box, a beautiful piece of
Moorish inlaid work, to within my easy reach, and then drawing a
deep breath of smoke, began:

"I started life about as low as any new peer. My father was a Jew
and we lived in the Jewish quarter off the Commercial Road. When
he was sober he was very kind to me and my brothers. My mother
never had any great significance for me, but I realise now that she
must have been a very hard worked and hard treated woman as upon
her fell the sole burden of supporting her husband and large family.

"From the time when my first memories start I have always been
interested in drawing, and I used to use every scrap of paper and
every stump of pencil I could find, but lines never satisfied me — I
wanted colours and tones. And these I could not afford. Coloured
chalks used to be my chief delight and I used to take them from the
desk of the Rabbi who managed the local synagogue and to whom I

used to go once a week for religious inst[ruction?]. For my father, though quite indifferu[e]nt[1] himself, was always most particular that I should attend. The Rabbi used the chalks, I remember, to draw maps of the divisions of the tribes with.

"Well one day he caught me taking his chalks, but instead of beating me, as the red-haired master at the board school would have done, he asked me all about my drawing and finally persuaded me to let him take some of my work away to show to his rich friends. For he was the son of a very rich man himself and had been to the 'Varsity but had sacrificed it all to help his fellow countrymen in the slums. I tell you that there are just as fine acts of self-sacrifice done by the rabbis in the Yiddish quarter as by any of your parsons at Kennington, only they don't brag about it.

["]Well, he showed my work to his friends in the West, with the result that a few days later a man [last five words of sentence moved to this position] came to [the] door and asked to see me and my work with a top hat and spats. He gave half-crowns to all my brothers but he didn't give my[e] half a crown, and I remember, I was very offended until I heard that I was to be taken away and taught painting.

["]That was the beginning of my 'career.' Those Jews ran me for the next five years, and I painted just as I was told to at the Academy school, to which I was sent. And everyone was very kind to me and I was introduced to lots of rich men, not only the moneyed Jews but men of your class who spend lots of money on being bored and are called [last five words of sentence moved to this position] 'in society' by lower middle class novelists. I began to acquire social polish and was being shaped into a pretty little gentleman; but all the time particularly when I could feel the grain of the canvas under my brush, I was dissatisfied.

["]When I was nineteen they gave me a studio, nothing like this, of course, but a decent enough shed with a good north light — and set me up as a Society portrait painter. Well I painted and flattered the ugly old women, that came to me, for a time; but after a little I found I could stand it no longer. I was painting badly, insipidly, insincerely, and I knew I could do better. I saw that the whole Academic conception was false — yes, that sounds funny from me nowadays, doesn't it? But we all see things more clearly when we're young.

["]That autumn the Italian futurists came to London and Ma-

---

[1] Penciled corrections and comments by master indicated in brackets.

rinetti delivered his epock[h] making series of broken-English lectures at the Dorée galleries. It was there, and particularly in Severini's ball-room scenes, that I found what I and half Chelsea had been looking for.

["]I always acted on impulses then, and when I came back and found in my room the luggage I had been packing for a tour through Italy with the Jews, — they still ran me, though by that time I was making a fairly decent living—I was filled with revulsion. I wrote a brief, I am afraid rude, note to them, and slamming the door of my studio rushed out into the night.

"I have no clear idea of what happened that night. I went to the Cafée [second *e* canceled] Royal and dru[a]nk absinthe. And soon I joined a group at the next table and together, as the sham English Bohemians do, we drank a lot, & laughed a lot, and finally all reeled out into the cool air of Regent Street. There were girls with us too, who had their hair cut short though it was not fashionable then. The leader of the set was a beautiful youth with red-gold hair whom we all called Ronald. I never learned his sirname though I met him continually for the next year and shared his studio with him. He painted fierce warm-colored 'abstractions' in tremendous bouts of energy which left him lethargic and apathetic. He was a great friend of mine in the year I spent in our sham Quartier Latin. For after that night I left the Jews and spent my time with the young art students and futurists. We were a happy enough lot and I should always have looked back to that year as the best of my life if—

"Well, during that year I painted as I have never painted before or since. I painted as I knew I ought to[,] without convention or restraint. I exhibited at the Mansard Gallery and in the Adelphi and reviews of my work appeared in 'Blast' and 'The Gypsy.' I was gloriously happy in my work & then it was all spoilt, and by a woman.

"I won't say much about that, if you don't mind. I was desperately in love and Ronald kept telling me not to be a fool. I wouldn't listen to him and began to break with my friends. She was a model and her vision remains to me now as the most beautiful thing I need ever fear to see. . . . Well, the crash came, as Ronald said it would, and I tore up all my drawings and stuffed the stove in the studio full of them. And I sc[r]aped the paint off my canvases with my palette knife; and I had one tremendous night with the whole set 'flung roses, roses, riotously with the throng, seeking to put thy pale lost lilies out of my mind.' We were all very noisy and drunk and we told

Rabellaisian jokes till far into the morning, and then in the grey of dawn I slunk back to the respectability and the Jews."

He was speaking, up till now, very seriously and bitterly. Now he shook his great shoulders like a dog, tossed his head, & motioning me to resume my pose took up his palette.

"Oh yes, they received me with open arms. And Mayfair accepted me as it's season's attraction. The old life went on. They made me an R.A. and—Happy? why yes. Why not? I've made a good thing out of life. Ask any of your club friends, they'll tell you so. But there are times when I see reviews of Ronald's work and hear my academic colleagues' sneers of him that I—Oh well; we must get on with the damned picture while the light lasts."

23

The House:
An Anti-Climax

[Undated, but internal evidence places it after mid-March, 1921, when Waugh's rebellion against the authorities in general and the Officer Training Corps in particular came to a head. See *A Little Learning,* pp. 131–35, and *Diaries,* pp. 116–21. Text: Manuscript in the Humanities Research Center, *Catalogue,* A7.]

[Very good. You should try your hand at something more serious next time. 27/30][1]

Never, in it's varied and not always unqualifiedly succesful career, had the school been in a state of such utter disorganisation and prostration, as in the Easter term, 1917. In France & Flanders, our thinly gaurded [error marked], inadequately munitioned lines, were quite incapable of successfully resisting the menaced German "push," every paper brought news of further mis-management and ill-success, every post news of some friend or relation who had been killed. At school, the houses had mostly been taken over, in the absense of their younger housemasters, by well meaning but incompetent elderly assistant masters; the prefects were young, and knowing that in a few weeks, at the most a few months, they would be "called up" to go to possible death, almost certain mutilation, cared little for school or house affairs. All over the country nerves were strained to the breaking point. This must be borne in mind when reading a story which at any other period would have been utterly impossible.

Every house, of course, claims to be the best, and in all probability has hypnotised itself into believing so, but there is one House that is more exclusive, more arrogantly self-confident, more self contained, than any other. The House has many exclusive points of

---

[1] Penciled corrections and comments indicated in brackets.

etiquette that the out-houses look on with contempt or resentment. They have largely their own slang, a great many of their own customs, and above all an unshakable contempt for the corps and all its machinations. Every flight of Inspection-day oratory leaves them the same, and even when all over the country militarism was all powerful, when soldiers drilled on the Christ Church quads at Oxford, they kept up their contempt with unmitigated bitterness. And then came Ross. A prefect, an excellent all round athlete, with a high place in the Classical sixth, he had remained quite a nonentity until he returned at the beginning of the Easter term to find himself head of the House, now demoralised and bereft of all its earlier dignity.

He had to take the entire management of the House into his own hands, and very soon he made himself felt. He stopped people getting "orders" for confectionary from their temporary house master, he stopped people getting leaves of [marked with × in margin] Clubs & Parades without consulting the matron at all, he generally raised the house to something like it's former standard and on the whole people liked it, for fundamentally men rather like being kept in order if it is done in the right way.

For the first three weeks all went well — too well really. Then came the Monday afternoon parade in which the corps started organising for the House Platoons Shield. Ross delivered a violent little speech and, as in most of his speeches, he said rather more than he meant to. "Stand easy and pay attention. The display that you have given so far has been perfectly monstrous. I've never seen such marching in my life before — might be a whole lot of boy scouts. I can tell you, that if you think that because this House has been disgustingly slack in the past, you are going to be disgustingly slack now, you are quite wrong for once in your lives. You're going to sweat for this — sweat your guts out — and I'm going to make you! Got that?" and he called the platoon up.

The House looked on him with undiguised [error marked in pencil] amazement and disgust and slowly meandered through the platoon drill with their customary negligence.

Next Tuesday's uniform parade saw the House with tarnished buttons, mud caked boots, and fouled rifles as usual. Next day saw the whole platoon doing "defaulters."

And so it went on, and gradually the House began to give way to his personality and even attained a certain sullen efficiency when suddenly a few days after the House Trials, an occurrence happened which altered the whole complexion of affairs.

One afternoon Ross was sitting in the house captain's room reading, when Stewart burst in, in running change, rather dirty, obviously just returned from a run.

Stewart was captain of Running and certain, people said, to be, at any rate, in the first three in the Five Mile — very possibly a winner.

He sat down on the window seat and began idly fingering the congealing mud on his knees. Then he looked up. "Ross," he said in the drawl always affected by prefects & house captains in the House, "I suppose you know that you are playing hell with the House, with your corps-mania?" Ross said nothing but pushed his book onto the table after carefully marking the place. After a pause Stewart went on.

"The House hasn't got either the time or inclination to do you [error marked in pencil] beastly corps, and clubs properly. We've no chance for the Footer, I know, but we've got a damned good chance for the Five Mile Jerry; and we aren't going to throw it away to play soldiers."

Still Ross said nothing; only the corners of his mouth moved.

"Well to give you an example. I told young Merrivale that I wanted him for a training run today and he said that he had to clean his bayonet to show to you before hall, because it was rusty yesterday. I said I would make it all right with you, of course, but I can't train a team decently if your beastly bayonets are going to get in the way every minute."

Then Ross spoke. "I'm sorry to dissapoint [errors marked in pencil] you, but Merrivale's bayonet has got to be cleen [error marked in pencil] before he goes for any run.

Stewart was genuinely astounded. "D'you mean to say you put your ruddy platoon shield before the Five Mile Jerry?" he demanded.

"You put it rather crudely" drawled Ross, "but that is what, I suppose, it comes to eventually."

Then Stewart lost his temper. "There's one thing you're forgetting" he said, "and that's that I'm not going to try and train a team with you getting in my light all the time. I'm a house-captain and needn't run if I don't want to. If you don't chuck your corps-mania I shan't run in the five-mile."

Stewart of course meant this as a threat that could not be argued against, the idea that he would be taken at his word was unthinkable, as indeed in a cooler moment it would have been to Ross. But now he was out to score. "Then I suppose Caven will have to run after all — he's first spare man isn't he?"

They had both made a decision which the [error marked] knew quite well would be dissastrous [error marked] but now neither could withdraw. Stewart, who had a great sense for the dramatic, went straight to the house board and crossed himself off the head of the list in a breathless silence.

The news spread round the House and then round the school with Oriental speed. The out-houses were openly exultant, the House sullen. Why, they asked, should they lose a cup, just because the bloods quarreled. They split up into factions and argued incessantly. Ross had missed the House trials in the last two years & no one new [error marked] his capabilities as a runner, but he immediately began to train rigorously, and people soon saw that he meant to win the house the cup without Stewart, who watching with the appreciation of the connoisseur, saw that he was a very fine runner. The house settled down to watch the five mile as the settling of the feud.

Stewart, very repentant, came down in a great coat to watch the finish. The House did not win.

Personality and will can do as much as the Pelme[?]n advertisements say, but they cannot force the pace up the Cow-Top and then lead a quarter mile sprint to Combs. A huddled heap after the Valley dyke were [marked in pencil] all that was left of Ross's training.

A week late came the house Platoons competition and muffled up and very white Ross came down from the San to watch. He was bitterly conscious of his failure and wondering how he would be able to endure another term of the cold superiority of Stewart and the glowering animosity of the whole House.

But suddenly he saw that the House Platoon were drilling as they had never drilled before or — thank God! — have since. Public opinion is the most unaccountable thing in the world and with his failure had suddenly come a popularity that he would never have enjoyed before had he been triumphant. The House, in their own great way were showing him their change of opinion. Their equipment was clean, and under Stewart as platoon commander they were drilling with an enthusiasm which went far to counteract the effect of the lethargy of their previous efforts.

It would make a splendid ending if the House could be allowed to win the Shield, but this is a story of school life and anyone who knows the House will know that that is out of the question. Suffice it to say, however, that they were third, and that as Ross went down the grass slope to Chapel that evening, arm in arm with Stewart it seemed almost as if he had forgiven the House rather than that they had forgiven him. And after all that is greatness.

24

The Return
of Launcelot

[In Waugh's diary entry for February 27, 1921, Waugh noted, besides a visit from Alec and his wife, that "I have thought of an idea for the Prize Poem. Spenserean stanzas on any incident in Malory. Bedivere when Arthur is dead and Lancelot sums things up cynically but not very bitterly. It's all over, things like that don't last. Men aren't like that really. Unfortunately this is not 'narrative.'" On vacation, early in April, he was trying to "cultivate the habit of working at night. Besides the fact that it appeals to my imagination, it is the only time when the house is at all quiet." However, the poem was not going well:

> As sometimes walking in the middle of London one has a sudden impulse to run, I feel that I must write prose or burst. I have been tinkering away for two hours, and shall not sleep unless I can clear my brain. To express oneself in the Spenserian stanza is as though one had to paint a picture on little bits of paper and fit them together like a jigsaw puzzle.
>
> I am doing badly. I have only done about half a dozen verses and most of them are complete balls. I find myself forced into the most hideous rhymes. [*Diaries,* pp. 114, 123; see also *A Little Learning,* p. 137]

For a contemporary reaction to the poem, see Dudley Carew, *A Fragment of Friendship* (London: Everest Books, 1974), pp. 28–29. Text: Manuscript in the Humanities Research Center, *Catalogue,* B9.]

English Verse:

   by

"Lavernia Scargill."

"Tut, Tut, child! there's a moral in everything if only you can find it."

Evelyn Waugh, Apprentice

The Return of Launcelot after the Siege of Joyous Gard.
Malory: Book 21, chapters VIII, IX, X

Told by Sir Bors, now in the holy land, many years later

Arthur is dead and Guinever his Queen;
Gawain for hate, Tristram for love lie slain;
And Launcelot, than whom was never seen
A knight more kingly, many years has lain
Entombed at Joyous Gard, for whom Elaine
Died in the tower of wind swept Astolot.
And I, Sir Bors, ride on this glaring plain
With stumbling horse and armour burning hot,
Who knew the fields of summer scented Camelot.

More than Elaine or Guinever could know
Or his pale hearted, priestly Galahad,
We loved Sir Launcelot; and years ago
at Joyous Gard we all of us, half clad
In what the moment offered, danced like mad
About him and from round the panelled wall
Stripped down the blazoned flags — such dreams we had
That night — and shouted till the vaulted hall
Rang with it, and he smiled, Godlike, upon us all.

I am grown old and have forgotten much;
That night lives still though all our dreams are dead.
Sleepless I lay and, now and then, would touch
With my hot hand the armour by my bed
Or feel the cross that hung above my head
And mutely pray for dawn. When, hard and clear
A trumpet woke the night, the measured tread
Below the windows stopped. With sudden fear
The castle stiffened, like an hound-awakened deer.

And then again, insistent, clear and loud
The challenge echoed in the outer night.
Into the Keep I joined the growing crowd
And with them jostled in the dancing light.
We strained and leaped seeking to gain a sight;
Someone had entered by the Northern Gate;
To him we surged, steel girded for the fight
And joined wild voiced in surmise & debate;
And over us stood Launcelot, silent calm and great.

And then he spoke and with his arm upraised
Moved us to instant silence. "We have fought
"A year against our King. Now, God be praised!
"This feud is at an end with all it brought
"Of death and ravin. Once more Arthur's court
"Shall welcome Launcelot; the towers shall ring
"with cheers, flag-decked for tournament & sport.
"Arthur has need of us. Now we can bring
"To aid him arms illused against our Lord & King.

"Gawaine is dead, slain by the wound I gave
"In battle before Benwick. Ere he died,
"He sent this message, that he now forgave
"That wrong I did his house, and dying cried
"for my forgiveness on that bitter pride
"which cleft the court of Arthur; and he told
"How Mordred over England far and wide
"Had raised revolt and Arthur's Kingly hold
"was weakened, and his son reigned arrogant and bold.

"The world is well again! Soon we shall feast
"with all our peers about the table round.
"Goodwill and Peace will come for man & beast
"And we shall hunt and gallop, flower crowned
"And joust upon Tintagagel's tented ground.
"Bright Camelot shall shine with silken dress
"Damasc and tapestry, with gold threads bound,
"Banners shall blaze more bright than we can guess
"And all the countryside shall carol happiness."

So dreamed we all and feasted, till we saw
The bladed steel of dawn cleave through the sky;
then soberly began the work of war.
The painted ships, with pennons waving high
High heaped with all our shining armoury
Before the noon, swept from the coast of France.
There shines about us the proud pageantry
of flags and banners streaming from each lance,
And round the ship hung out the brave escutcheons dance.

Oh passing brave our shew and passing sweet!
The blue waves dashed to white about our bow.
Launcelot paced with slow, unhurried feet,
Now smiling at some hidden thought and now

Straining his gaze before him, seeing how
The low cliffs slowly whitened more and more
Now at the rush of foam behind the prows
As on and ever on our gay fleet bore
Until at length our keels ground on the Dover shore.

The sun was setting, grey and desolate;
Slowly great drops of rain began to fall.
The flags hung lifeless and with sullen weight
Our cloaks clung to our armour, and we all
Huddled for shelter in the buttressed wall.
Red in the west our day of promise died.
"Open to Launcelot," rang our heralds call;
Silence; and then the sound of feet inside
And on the battlements a figure rose and cried,

"Begone, Begone! We've had enough of arms
"Merchants we want, not chivalry and Knights
"and rival Kings who pillage towns and farms.
"We have no part in all your wars and fights
"Begone, my Lords! We townsmen have our rights
"as well as you. Unless you come with gold,
"You cannot come. Ours are the market lights;
"If you bring ought that may be bought or sold,
"Enter. If not remain without and fight the cold."

Then cried Sir Launcelot, "Are things thus changed
"Since Galahad from Camelot rode out
"White armoured; and in green Sir Tristram ranged
"The country round with tournament and bout,
"That tradesmen rise and from their ramparts shout
"Thus at their lords? Come down! or when I've paid
"Vengeance for Gawaine in Sir Mordred's rout,
"I'll teach you manners in the gallows shade
"And shew you in the flames how Launcelot is obeyed."

"That may you not, Sir Knight, for know you well
"The age of knights is over. He who buys
"now rules. For in the west King Arthur fell
"And with him all his knightly army lies.
"This is the age of shops and merchandise!"
Launcelot spoke not, only turned his head
And with his hand covered his Kingly eyes.
"Those are they last words, slave" Sir Gareth said
And seized a bow and shot the sneering townsman dead.

And Launcelot pacing on the wind swept down
As we set up our tents against the rain
And, looking back upon the lighted town
Said, "Much is lost, but some things still remain.
"This day, at least, has wiped away that stain
"That marred my love for Guinever. Now I
"Shall lead her back to Joyous Gard again.
"The world's still good, though much good pass us by."
His only answer was the distant sea bird's cry.

Early at morning Launcelot rode forth.
We watched him from the hillside as he went
Erect, alone, into the misty north;
Then turning sadly walked from tent to tent
With dreary whisperings and shoulders bent.
But Launcelot rode ever night and day
In fruitless search, till hopeless, lost & spent
He struck upon a moss grown forest way
And came at last to Almesbury where a convent lay.

And, seeking rest he rode towards the door;
A hooded nun answered the turret bell;
"Good nun," he said, "a weary knight and poor
Comes to you friendless. Now, I pray you, tell,
Know you where went the Queen when Arthur fell?"
And as he spoke, a cry rang soft and clear;
He turning saw a nun outside her cell
Surrounded by her maids and drawing near
Launcelot fell before the feet of Guinever.

Then spake she, "Ladies, through this man and me
"Hath all this long disastrous war been wrought.
"And through our love fell Arthur's chivalry
"And all his nob[l?]est knights. And we have brought
"The death of my most noble Lord. Then ought
"we, by that mighty love which once we knew
"never to meet again. But I in thought
"And penance for our grievous sin, and you
"In feudal duties, should we start our lives anew."

And Launcelot made answer, "Never fear
"That Launcelot like Tristram shall take wife
"When he has known the love of Guinever.
"I have lived well in tournament and strife;

"Now seek I rest; 'tis all I ask of life.
"But ere I tread that unaccustomed way,
"Once more recall the time when love was rife,
"When blood was hot, and armour lit the fray;
"Grant me one kiss to seal our lasting love today."

"Nay, Launcelot, that shall I never do.
"Greatly we loved and great has been our fall;
"And so I tell you, as that love was true
"It now lies dead without the Convent wall,
"With all that world, which I would not recall.
"Heaven takes it's toll of those who serve it best."
And Launcelot turned and mounting left them all
Unseeing, rode into the glowing West
And all the night he galloped headlong without rest.

At dawn his horse dropped senseless & he fell
Upon the cool dewscented grass and lay
Sightless with grief, until a sacring bell,
Ringing for Masse, greeted the silver day.
And then he looked and saw not far away
A little altar circled by a belt
of elm trees; and he rose and went to pray.
Before the cross an aged hermit knelt.
"Here I can find that peace I seek" Launcelot felt.

And after Masse the old man turned to him
And peering said, "What make you here, good knight,
Covered with mud and dust in every limb?
Perhaps you come from some far-rumoured fight
With news of victory, that all the night
You ride thus recklessly." Launcelot said
Sadly in answer, "Would that you were right.
"I come defeated, who before ne'er fled,
"And all I seek is where to lay my weary head.

"Much have I seen, which I must now forget;
"I have been great, and not unknown to fame;
"And now I ride alone, weary and wet
"And slaves and peasants spit upon my name.
"With waving flags and dancing dreams I came;
"I sought to see the world well-made at last.
"To me this life has always been a game
"Where I have played & won; now that is passed
"And all I seek is rest, with penance & with fast."

So when at length we sought Sir Launcelot,
Fearing to find him in some dungeon caught
Or slain by enemies, we found him not;
But up and down the country vainly sought,
Till, turning back, one of our squires brought
News of an hermit, who, with patient Art
Could see into the future and had wrought
Great wonders and much good through all that part,
And Hector said, "Let us consult him ere we start."

And when we found him, thus he answered us
"Good knights, Sir Launcelot is living yet,
"But he has found by means tempestuous
"That goal to which all human paths are set;
"He would not tread that path again. Forget
"The man you knew, but seek his lonely road."
And as he spake, he knelt in prayer and let
His cowl fall back and to the sunset shewed
The head of Launcelot which in red splendour glowed.

Then said the hermit, "I am very old
"And have learned much alone. The wild herd's bleat
"All the shy magic of the winter's cold
"And the fierce pageantry of summer's heat
"Have taught me more of man than any feat
"of arms or horse upon the battle plain.
"And this I learned: the world is not more sweet
"For man's good acting, nor for human pain
"More ugly, nor more wise for any human brain.

"When you had hope, you cried, 'The world is good,'
And when your hope proves false, you ride alone
"And cry 'The world is ill,' and in this wood
"Fall down and ask for Rest. But I was shewn
"At night among the reeds and grasses blown,
"The world is neither good nor bad, and Rest
"Abides as much in forest, down and stone
"And may be met in crowds. Those are the blessed
"Who find it in themselves alone and guard it best."

[The play was in rehearsal by June 13; Waugh and E. B. Gordon, the house-tutor, had printed the invitations on Saturday, June 11. It was produced on June 17 and 20, according to the diary entries. The Epilogue mentioned in the diary has apparently not survived. See *Diaries*, pp. 127–29; Arthur Waugh, *One Man's Road* (London: Chapman and Hall, 1931), p. 369; and Dudley Carew, *A Fragment of Friendship: A Memory of Evelyn Waugh When Young* (London: Everest Books, 1974), pp. 24, 30–32, 36–37. Text of the play: Typescript in Humanities Research Center, *Catalogue*, B10. Text of the Epilogue: Carew: *A Fragment of Friendship*, p. 36.

Act 1 is a parody of numberless school stories; act 2 parodies Alec Waugh's *The Loom of Youth*; act 3 is obviously based on Waugh's ragging of the Officer Training Corps, described in *A Little Learning* (Boston: Little, Brown, 1964), pp. 131–35, and *Diaries* (pp. 116–21, March 11–18, 1921). See also Editor's Introduction.]

The Headmaster's House
requests the honour of your company
on Sunday, June 19th, at 7:45 p.m. in
The Great School at a performance of

Conversion

the tragedy of youth in three burlesques

by
Evelyn Waugh

Act I. School, as maiden Aunts think it is.
Act II. School, as modern authors say it is.
Act III. School, as we all know it is.

R.S.V.P., F. E. Ford

Act I.

School as Maiden Aunts think it is.

Characters

Dr. Grimthorpe.	The Head.	
Jenkins.	The hero.	
Simmonds.	His friend.	} good boys.
Smith.	A new boy.	
Sloper.	The School Bully.	} bad boys.
Toad.	His crony.	

Scene. Dr. Grimthorpe's Academy for the education of the sons of Gentlemen

Enter Jenkins and Simmonds.

Jenkins.   Well, Simmonds, isn't it grand to be back at the old school once more?

Simmonds.   Yes, Jenkins. We have a great school tradition. I am very proud of these old grey stones.

J.   But you must not think that I am in any way insensible to the refining influence of the holidays. I feel the spell of home affection always keeps me from sloth and sensual snares.

S.   How true, Jenkins. You are always so profound. And what pure and blameless pleasures have you enjoyed since we last met?

J.   I have had on the whole a quiet holidays. Once my kind aunt took me to the Cinematograph to see the pictures of the flight to Australia. Those are the only sort of films she will see.

S.   And, I think, rightly. If one can combine instruction with pleasure, then all is well.

J.   Always provided, of course, that instruction is not used as a mere cloak for indulgence.

S.   How true. It must be wonderful to be as clever as you.

J.   If I am any service to you, I find it most gratifying, Simmonds. As a matter of fact the Doctor's wife told me last term, when I had the privelege of having tea with her, that

95

she considers that I am as great an influence for good at
Grimthorpe House as Sloper is for ill.

S.   Then does she know that Sloper is the School bully?

J.   I think she must suspect it. (Noise outside.) But hush, I
think this must be he.

Enter Sloper.

How do you do, Sloper? I hope that your holidays have been
improving.

Sloper.   Hullo, you chaps. Have a drink. I've got a bottle of gin
in my box. Or lay a bet with me. I can tell you a dead cert.;
Old Tay Bridge for the Grand National.

J.   No, Sloper, thank you.

Sl.   I say, don't get batey.

J.   I am not angry, Sloper, only bitterly disappointed. I had
hoped to see you a better boy since your Confirmation.

Sl.   Oh, Confirmaggers hasn't done anything.

J.   Sloper, after a piece of blasphemy such as that, the best thing
you can do is to go. You need not threaten me, sir. You may
be the School bully, but you know that you are afraid of me.

Exit Sloper.

I hope I was not unreasonably violent with him. I find him
very disappointing. How could he speak like that after the
Bishop's address.

S.   Is there no influence that will touch his heart?

J.   There must be somewhere.

Enter Dr. Grimthorpe and a new boy, Smith.

Dr. G.   Jenkins, Simmonds, let me introduce you to Smith. He
is to be one of your comrades this term.

J.   Welcome to Grimthorpe House, Smith.

S.   How do you do? I am glad that you have come to share with
us our boons of study and leisure.

Dr. G.   I will leave him in your hands, boys. I particularly wish
him to be treated well. Do not let Sloper bully him.

J.   I will in all my best obey you, Dr. Grimthorpe.

Exit Dr. Grimthorpe.

Well, Smith, I hope that your Mother and Father are well.

Smith.   Yes, thank you, sir.

J.   Come, come, you mustn't call me "Sir." We are all friends here. Call me Jenkins.

Sm.   Yes, Jenkins. *(Noise without.)*

J.   But hush, here comes Sloper again and with one of his cronies.

Enter Sloper with Toad.

Sloper.   Ah, here's a go. Toad, here is a new chap.

Toad.   Good, let us make game of him.

J.   I don't like the looks of Sloper.

Sl.   Good evening, new boy.

Sm.   Good evening.

Sl.   Say "Sir" when you speak to me.

T.   And stand up properly when you speak to Sloper.

Sm.   I'm sorry, sir.

Sl.   That's better. Now then, what's your name?

Sm.   Charles Arbuthnot Millicent Courtnay Philip Smith, sir.

Sl.   Good Lord, where did you get a name like that from?

Sm.   My godfathers and my godmothers in my baptism, wherein I was made—

Sl.   Don't quote that stuff to me, blast you. I had to learn that for—

J.   Not that blasphemous name again, Sloper, in the presence of a new boy.

Sl.   Oh, Confirmation then. Though I don't see what it has got to do with you.

J.   I have promised the Doctor to take care of him.

Sl.   Oh, you did, did you? Well, young mollycoddle, what's your father?

Sm.   I cannot tell you, sir.

Sl.   What, do you refuse?

Sm.   I do.

Sl.   Am I thwarted?

Sm. You are.

T. Shall I fill a bath with boiling water, Sloper?

Sl. Yes, you might—or wait. We must get rid of Jenkins first. I can't stand a hero about when I have to bully.

T. I think I can do it. Jenkins and Simmonds, I think the Doctor wants you.

S. When did he say that?

T. Just before we came in. I forgot to mention it before.

J. I hate leaving Smith in their hands. But still—come on.

Exit Jenkins and Simmonds.

Sl. Well done. You are a clever chap. Now to work. Come here!

Sm. Yes, sir.

Sl. Do you still defy me?

Sm. I must still keep from you the knowledge of my father's occupation, but not from any sort of disagreeableness, I assure you.

T. That remains to be seen.

Sl. Why won't you tell me?

Sm. I can't.

Sl. Can't! Don't you know?

Sm. Yes, I know, but—

Sl. Then you lied to me. If you know, you can tell me.

Sm. But—

Sl. We'll soon show you how we treat liars at Grimthorpe House.

Sm. I promised not to, sir.

Sl. I can't help that, I'm afraid. For the last time, will you or will you not tell me?

Sm. I cannot say.

Sl. All right. Toad, get the red hot poker.

Sm. Oh! Don't hit me with that.

Sl. I will give you one more chance. What is your father?

Sm.   *(bursting into tears)* Well, if you must know, my father is in prison.

Enter Jenkins and Simmonds.

J.   So it was all a ruse, was it? The Doctor had not asked for us at all.

S.   What have you been doing to Smith in the meantime?

Sl.   Nothing.

J.   Nothing? Then why is he crying, and what are you doing with that poker? By heaven, you shall pay for this.

Sl.   I never touched him. I swear I never touched him.

J.   Simmonds, will you hold my coat for me? Toad, perhaps you will take Sloper's.

Fight. Sloper is knocked down.
Enter Dr. Grimthorpe.

Dr. G.   What, pray, is the meaning of this unseemly brawl? It looks to me as if you had been bullying again, Sloper.

J.   Yes, sir, I have just thrashed him. I caught him red-handed.

Dr. G.   Thank you, Jenkins. that is what I should have expected from you. And you, sir, what excuse can you offer for your dastardly conduct?

Sl.   Well, if you must know, John Jenkins, this kid, whom you take it upon you to protect, is the son of a jail-bird.

Sensation.

S.   This is a serious accusation you make, Sloper. Smith, say it is not true.

Sm.   It is true. My father has got three years penal.

T.   So you see who you've been protecting so jealously.

J.   Smith, I am only pleased that so good a chap as you can come from even the criminal classes.

Dr. G.   Allow me to speak. You may well say that, Jenkins. When you have heard all, you will think more of him. Jenkins, Simmonds, Sloper, Toad, and Smith, I feel that some explanation is due to you all. This boy, whom you have so basely ill-used, is the son of a most honourable man. His father, to save another man who was being convicted of theft, went to the Judge and told him that he had done the crime. The Judge believed him and he is now doing three years for another man. That man, Sloper, is your father.

Sl. Oh! *(Sinks into a chair.)*

Dr. G. Come, boy, receive the punishment you have so richly deserved.

Sm. Sir, I beg you to forgive this unfortunate boy. I feel that I may be able to convert him. He is not so bad as his face would lead you to think. As you are strong, sir, be merciful.

Dr. G. (touched). Well Sloper, I feel you are unworthy of this lad's mediation, but since he asks it, I will spare you. Toad, I will birch you instead. Come.

Exit Dr. Grimthorpe and Toad.

J. This is the influence that will reform Sloper.

S. Let us leave them together.

Exit Jenkins and Simmonds.

Sm. Sloper.

Sl. Don't speak to me. I am not worthy of you.

Sm. Sloper, did you ever have a mother?

Sl. No, my mother died many years before I was born.

Sm. My poor fellow! But you have an Aunt.

Sl. Yes. How did you guess?

Sm. I thought there must be some redeeming quality even in your nature. When you say a bad word, or bully a little boy, what would your aunt say?

Sl. I never thought of that.

Sm. You must always think of that, Sloper. Before you do anything, say to yourself, "What would Auntie say?"

Sl. I will, I will. Oh, how can I thank you?

Sm. Do not thank me, Sloper. Try and be better.

Sl. You are a good chap to me, Smith. I'm not worth it.

Sm. No, but I hope some day you will be. Come!

Exeunt.

Curtain.

Act II.

School, as Modern Authors Say It Is.

Characters.

Laurence	*An Athlete.*
Leighton.	*do.*
Pointer	*do.*
Collier	*do.*
Farquarson.	*An Intellectual.*
Mr. Tadema.	*A Master.*

The scene is laid in Fernhurst, one of the largest and wickedest of our Public Schools. Time, the evening before a house match. Laurence, Leighton, and Pointer are pacing the stage, tearing their hair.

Laurence.   I tell you we must win.

Leighton.   We've simply got to.

Pointer.   My God, if we don't!

La.   Sometimes before a House match I feel I could almost pray.

Le.   You don't exactly pray on the field, do you?

La.   Well, everyone swears at the referee in a first fifteen match, don't they?

P.   Jolly unsporting of the Head to birch you, I think.

Le.   They'll be turning you off the field for fouling next.

P.   Oh, they couldn't possibly do that.

La.   They might, you know. They're getting absurdly particular, confound them.

Le.   Yes, Millais sent Watts off the field the other day for punching in the scrum.

La.   Absurd.

Le.   As if it wasn't a regular tradition of Fernhurst football to foul in the scrum.

P.   Well, the Head's on our side anyway. He said to me in Chapel this morning, "Don't let one of those God-forsaken Dunkin's men come out alive."

La.   Splendid fellow he is. I loathe all this cant about

101

sportsmanship. Everyone knows that one goes on the field to fight — even the referee.

Le. Pretty state Fernhurst football would be getting into if we started playing like gentlemen.

La. Lord, yes!

P. D'you remember Collier in the Tonwich match? The way he brought down that back.

Le. Oh, it was wonderful. He's a wonderful chap, if you like.

La. Yes, he may be half-witted and a cad, and he may not wash, but he's got a wonderful hand-off.

P. If only we had some more people like him in the House.

La. I'm told he steals a good deal.

Le. What does that matter if he's good at football?

P. If we had another Collier instead of Farquarson.

La. I believe I caught Farquarson preparing the construe this morning.

P. Oh rot, I can't believe that of him. He may be pretty awful, but —

La. I'm almost certain I saw him.

Le. Oh come, you shouldn't say a thing like that behind a man's back. He must have been using a crib.

La. No, it was a big Liddell & Scott.

Le. Good Lord!

P. Something's got to be done about this.

La. Before a House match too. *(Enter Collier. He looks depressed.)* Hullo, feeling in good form for to-morrow?

Collier. Don't speak to me about to-morrow. I shan't be playing.

La. Good God, they can't have turned you out.

C. I shan't be here to play.

La. Won't be here? What, has your pater gone bankrupt or something? You shouldn't let that sort of thing interfere with football, you know.

C. Oh, it's nothing like that. Fact is, I've got the push.

Le. Good Lord!

P. What for?

La. Stealing?

C. Yes, I suppose I was bound to be caught some day. I went to tea with Mrs. G. yesterday and stole the spoons. I don't think she noticed at the time, but the matron found them in my press this morning.

P. He hasn't given you the push for that?

Le. Before a House match.

La. What infernal luck.

P. I think he might have let you stay till to-morrow.

C. Oh, he was most emphatic about it. Said I was a corrupting influence, if you please. He only let me come and see you men because I told him I wanted to get an aspirin. I must go back in a second. I've got to catch the night train. Besides, I might corrupt you. Good God! I never stole anything before I came here. Fernhurst taught me to steal. I began by taking people's buns in Hall; then I stole someone's straw hat on Sunday afternoon; then I took stationery from the Secretary's office — I've got heaps of thick notebooks in my pit. Then I stole the fines money and any amount of Library books. After that I just took anything. I bagged half a dozen rifles from the Armoury last term; the Bandmaster got blamed. Fernhurst has taught me to steal, and now it says, "You're not fit to be a member of this great school." It's beastly unfair. Well, I must be going, I suppose. Cheerio, you men.

Exit.

La. Who on earth will play full-back now?

P. Why the deuce couldn't the man wait till we'd got the jerry?

Le. Our defence will be hopeless.

La. Dunkin's are sure to beat us now.

P. Lord, what an ass he was.

La. I suppose Turner'll have to play in his place.

P. Hunt will get past him every time.

Le. I suppose, in a way, it's rather bad luck on him too.

P. His whole life's pretty well ruined. He'll have to go out to the Colonies or somewhere.

La. Yes, I suppose so. But how on earth can you think of things like that when we're in danger of losing a Cup?

P. He couldn't have chosen a worse time.

La. Beastly unsporting of Mrs. G. to put her beastly spoons before a House Cup.

Le. You couldn't expect a woman to understand a thing like that.

P. They never think.

La. No sense of proportion.

Enter Collier with Farquarson

C. Hullo, you men. I had to come back again and bring this swine. I caught him going across the quad with a Virgil under his arm. That was more than I could stand, so I brought him back to deal with him.

La. Quite right.

Le. What were you doing with that Virgil, Farquarson.

Farquarson. Oh, go away, Leighton, I've got some work to do.

C. You hear him. I couldn't leave with that on my conscience.

P. I should think not. Farquarson, you weak-kneed, useless, inky, unwashed disgrace to the House. Come here, you sweaty beast.

F. Oh, please go away and be funny somewhere else. I must do this Virgil by to-night.

P. You must what?

C. Gentlemen, he is condemned out of his own mouth.

Le. What shall we do to him?

La. Take his books away. That's right. Now, Farquarson, can you tell me the names of the House team?

F. Oh, shut up. I'm busy.

La. (hitting him). Don't speak to me like that, you God-forsaken little tick. Stand up straight, man, you're not on parade now, Good Lord! There now, you look quite an athlete, Farquarson. *(Hits him.)* Now, can you tell me the names of the House team?

F. I don't know why you men should bully me like this. You know I lead just as scandalous a life as you do.

Le. What the Hell's the use of leading a scandalous life, if you're not good at games.

La. May I repeat my question?

F. Oh, I don't know.

La. Farquarson, I warn you to be careful. Who are going to play for the House to-morrow? I may begin to think that you don't know, and you know what that would mean, don't you, Farquarson?

F. Oh, there's you and Leighton and Pointer and — and Collier.

La. Wrong for one. *(Hits him.)* Go on, you miserable beast.

F. Oh, there's Watts — and — and — Oh, confound you, I don't know.

La. Gentlemen, do you hear that? After a masterly cross-examination I have elucidated that not only does the prisoner want to work, but he doesn't know the names of the House team.

C. What shall we do to him?

P. Fairly lay him out.

Le. Let's take him out on the quad and beat him.

La. Rather.

P. Come on.

F. Shut up.

Le. Don't talk to me, man.

C. Good-bye, you men, I expect I shall be gone when you come back.

Le. Oh, cheerio.

P. Best of luck.

La. Good-bye, old thing.

Exeunt.

Collier remains alone.

C. So sometimes, when the last of all our evenings
   Crowneth memorially the last of all our days,

Then falls thy shadow, Cynera. The darkness brings,
Roses and roses, wine and other things.
Slowly at evening the last brave lights expire.
Gently on dune and headland sinks the opal fire.

(Enter Mr. Tadema behind.)

But I am desolate and sick of an old passion:
I have been faithful to thee, Cynera, in my fashion.

(Head sinks in hands.)

Tadema. "I would not waken you, nay this is fitter." Tell me, who are you who quoted Dowson at Fernhurst?

C. I am Collier.

T. What, not the boy who has just been expelled?

C. Yes.

T. Why did you do it?

C. I can't help it. I have a pagan soul.

T. Have you, Collier? Oh, I am glad to hear you say that. I have searched all Fernhurst to find one. We have the legacy of Marlowe.

C. Webster —

T. Beaumont —

C. Fletcher —

T. Swinburne, de Maupassant, Dowson, Dostoievsky.

C. Yes, yes.

Mr. Tadema and Collier recite "Dolores" together.

C. Oh, isn't it great, glorious!

T. But how, after that, can you descend to stealing? Be like Caesar, who would not massacre a town, not because he thought it a great sin but because he thought it a little sin. Live portentously. Whenever you are going to do a mean thing, think of a chorus from Atalanta.

C. Yes, I will. It's a glorious thing to be a pagan. Wine and roses and desire.

Exeunt quoting.

Curtain

Act III.

Scene: A House Room. Time: 12:30 p.m.

Enter Lodge and Hassal.

Lodge.　Well, what d'you think'll happen about this morning's show?

Hassal.　You mean Townsend's

L.　Yes.

H.　The Man's a most infernal ass. The Head'll be pretty bored about it.

L.　Shouldn't be surprised if he got the push.

H.　It was rather witty all the same.

L.　Yes, rather.

H.　Well, you laughed at the time.

L.　Yes, at the time the whole of Chapel did, even most of the Gods; but I think it was rather bad form, you know.

H.　Perhaps it was really. Still I swear he's got guts.

L.　Oh, he's got guts all right.

Enter Warner.

I say, any news about Townsend?

Warner.　Pretty bad, I think. I saw Maine talking to the Head in the break.

L.　Did you know he was going to do it?

W.　Yes, as a matter of fact he told me about it several days ago.

H.　Why on earth did you let him? Surely you knew what a hell of a row it'ld mean.

W.　Well, I didn't really think he'd do it, and besides he's got rather a way of making things sound all right.

H.　You would be taken in by his sort of plausibility.

W.　Well, I should like to see what you'd have done. After all it wasn't any of my beastly business.

L.　I wonder if he is such an atheist as he makes out.

W.　No, I think he does it because he wants a good rag.

H.   Yes, and become conspicuous.

L.   Well, he's in for the devil of a row.

Enter Townsend.

H.   I think he deserves all he gets, too. *(Lodge kicks him. He sees Townsend, who advances into the room as if he hadn't heard.)*

Townsend.   Haven't the weekly bumphs come yet?

W.   Hullo, old thing. No, I don't think so.

L.   I saw them down at the Porter's lodge when I was getting the letters, they ought to be up by now.

H.   I expect they're in the House Captains' room. They keep them there all day.

L.   Yes, I daresay. *(Awkward silence. Townsend sits down in corner with paper.)*

W.   Who's going to win between Carpentier and Dempsey?

T.   Dunno.

H.   Ever seen a prize fight?

L.   No. Pretty filthy, I should think, isn't it? Some of the Boxing Competitions make me feel sick.

H.   Can't think why people go.

T.   Oh, they're plenty of people who enjoy any sort of a row here provided someone else gets hurt. *(Awkward silence)*

W.   What are the clubs this afternoon?

H.   House match, isn't there?

L.   Good Lord, is there really? Who against?

H.   Olds or Gibbs, I think.

W.   I thought we drew a bye.

H.   Oh, perhaps we did. Anything on the board about it?

L.   Oh, yes it seems to be to-day.

H.   Who's playing.

L.   Maine, Froude, Lecky, Townsend and all the usual gang.

W.   I wonder who'll win.

L.   I'm afraid they will.

H.   Bet you a bob they don't.

L.   Why? Are you in the know or something? Don't say you're getting keen on Clubs.

H.   Lord, no. I only thought that if I had a bet on it it might give me some interest in it. I can't stand another afternoon like those under-sixteens last term. It's pretty dull and if one can't get worked up one gets a cold.

Enter Froude.

Hullo, you look pretty dejected. Have you been ragging the Chapel too?

Froude.   Oh, shut up.

W.   What the Hell's up?

F.   Oh, nothing, it's only that I'm in such a fearful wind up about this afternoon.

L.   This afternoon? Oh, do you mean the House match? But why?

F.   They're playing me inside right to-day. I've only played centre before. God, I'm sure I shall make an ass of myself.

W.   Well, what if you do?

F.   Well, isn't that bad enough for you? The whole House watching, depending on me.

H.   My God, the arrogance of these footballers! D'you really suppose the House as a whole cares a curse what you do?

F.   Well, they jolly well ought to.

L.   Why in Heaven's name?

F.   Why, it's most fearfully unpatriotic, of course they ought to.

H.   There's a morbid strain in these aggressively healthy people. They love torturing themselves. They spend all their time straining their hearts, and then they aren't satisfied unless everyone takes a tremendous interest in them so as to give them moral suffering too.

F.   Oh, I know you think you're beastly clever. We just think that you're a waster. *(He picks up a paper.)*

H.   Lord, what a fool! And to think that only a few years ago the School was absolutely run by people like that. It's as if the "motor-bike fiends" owned the place.

L.   Or the philaleptic society.

H.   Philatelic, you mean.

L.   P'raps I do. I don't know anything about them, except that they put up notices on the fire board.

Enter Maine.

Maine.   Townsend, may I speak to you before you go across to Hall, please?

T.   Certainly, Maine. *(Exit Maine. Froude and Townsend talk in a corner.)*

L.   Now he's for it. What do you think'll happen to him?

W.   Common-roomed?

H.   Lord, no. He'll be lucky if he gets off with a birching.

W.   It's rather bad luck. You thought it funny at the time.

H.   Yes, I've heard that before. Lots of things would be funny which one can't do. At least anyone with a sense of proportion can't.

W.   Still I'm sorry for him.

L.   I don't see why you should be. He must have known it would mean a row when he arranged it.

H.   The man must have been a bit cracked, of course. He always loved playing to the gallery, and he hadn't the sense to see when he was going too far.

W.   You don't think he really felt strongly about the services?

L.   No, not for a moment. *(Exit Froude.)*

H.   I say, about this afternoon, we must get some food if we're going to watch this match. I suppose we're all watching together?

L.   Yes. Look here, will you double down to the Grubber immediately after Hall and get food for us all. About five bob's worth.

H.   Why can't you?

L.   I've got to get some money out.

W.   Dashed if I'm going to.

H.   Oh all right. Five bob's worth of anything?

L.   Yes, except those filthy cream bun things.

H.   Right you are. *("Stop talking" off.)*

W.   Oh, they're going in. Come across.

L.   Right. Wait a second. I must just get a paper.

H.   Come on, we don't want to be late.

Exeunt.

Townsend sits alone by the fire. Enter Froude.

F.   Hullo, I just came back for a book.

T.   Hullo.

F.   I suppose you're waiting to see Maine.

T.   Yes.

F.   What do you suppose will happen?

T.   Dunno.

F.   Well I'm jolly sorry for you, old thing. I think you've been making an ass of yourself, but I hope nothing much happens.

T.   Thanks awfully. The people I hate are those cads like Hassal. They were only too braced at the time, and now I'm in a row they think it's not done.

F.   Oh, he's one of those confounded intellectuals. Did you hear what he said about the House match?

T.   Yes.

F.   Thought himself beastly funny. You're playing this afternoon still, I suppose.

T.   I suppose so.

F.   Of course, cricket's really your game, but you've got a good chance of your House colours, and they're worth getting whatever Hassal says. Well, I must go across. Good luck.

T.   Thanks. *(Exit Froude.)*

Enter Maine. Both are a little awkward. He sits in front of the fire.

Maine.   Well, let's get to business. I suppose you know what I want to speak to you about.

T.   That Chapel show, I suppose.

M.   Yes. The Head has, very wisely I think, put the whole matter into my hands. He realised that prefects are naturally more in touch with the school and can discuss things more freely.

T.   I honestly don't think we shall gain anything by discussion, Maine. Please just tell me what you're going to do to me.

M. *(the prepared oration disturbed).*   Well—I—er. You can't force my hand like that, you know. One can't be so direct. Several issues are involved besides the mere matter of punishment. House politics and things. You can't be so direct.

T.   Do you mean you aren't going to tell me what you are going to do? Because, if so, it hardly seems worth while going on.

M.   My dear man, I don't know what is going to happen yet. It depends very largely on you.

T.   I should have thought I had done my share and it was now your turn.

M.   Look here, let me explain. This isn't an incident, it's an attitude. I can't just punish you and let the matter end with that, as I should if you were an underschool. You're one of the senior people in the House and one who I hope will soon be in an official position. Now you have taken up an attitude of deliberate opposition to a definite fact of the School System. Haven't you?

T.   Yes, I—

M.   Let me speak, please. Rightly or wrongly you have decided that the Chapel services are a farce and that the Christian religion is built on a lie.

T.   Yes, but—

M.   Please—Now supposing for the moment that you were right—I suppose there are some things which worry every man who thinks at all—do you think you would be justified in behaving as you have done? Let me just show you two other considerations. First, you may disapprove of religion, but there are a great many people to whom it means rather a lot, and even if you have not the tolerance you should at least have the courtesy to respect their views; secondly, when you came to the school you joined a definite institution of which the Chapel was one of the principal features. You join a community and you owe it the obligation to keep its rules.

T. Oh yes, you can bring out your arguments like a barrister. I've made speeches as good as that unprepared.

M. There's no need for impertinence, Townsend.

T. Oh, that's just the way. You say "Let us discuss things freely," and as soon as I begin to speak my mind you get on your dignity again.

M. We seem to be getting away from the subject. Now I'm not making much of this side of the question because I don't think that really you care either way.

T. That's just the way! Because you are slack and indifferent you think that no one can feel strongly about it. You think I must be frivolous and —

M. Now, don't get violent. Can you swear on your honour that it was real reforming fervour that made you do that show this morning?

T. No, of course, I can't. You know that well enough. It just gave me a romantic reason to keep me happy.

M. Then why did you do it? *(pause)*

T. Well, I don't really know. I think it was chiefly to get some incident into life. School is so frightfully dull. It is so easy to get into a rut and become self-important and content with little dignities. One has to do something to keep oneself sane.

M. Thanks. I'm glad you're honest with me.

T. There wasn't much to be gained by holding out, was there?

M. No, I think it was very sensible of you. Then that's settled.

T. What's settled?

M. Why that in future you'll adopt a sane attitude.

T. I never said anything about that.

M. Oh come, you can't keep it up now. I thought we understood one another.

T. D'you know, Maine, if you weren't a prefect I think I should call you a prig. You can't see that a person can go on deliberately doing anything without a high motive behind him. I don't intend to alter at all.

M.   Look here, Townsend, don't be a fool. D'you know what it will mean to quarrel with us?

T.   You can beat me.

M.   Yes, but we can do far more than that. We control everything that makes life tolerable to you. We can take away your pit and privileges, make you play in junior House games, take away all your dignity.

T.   I should still keep my self-respect.

M.   Don't think it. You'd lose that almost at once. It's no use taking up a heroic attitude. You're senior House colour for cricket now Stubbs has left. I suppose you want to be captain of the House next term?

T.   You can't alter that.

M.   No, but the Games Committee can. Now look here. I don't want you to think I'm blackmailing you or anything. Don't you understand that we can't have you in a position of authority like that if you persist in making an ass of yourself.

T.   I see.

M.   Now look here, it's getting awfully late for lunch. Do let's come to some understanding. If you will consent to lead a sane life, I'll let the whole matter drop. We shall be needing another House Captain next term and I shall recommend you. If not—You see I hold all the cards. Now, will you be sensible? *(pause)*

T.   All right.

M.   Good, that's splendid. I thought you would. Thank you.

Exit victorious. Townsend waits a second and then follows.

Curtain

Epilogue

If we offend you, in that we have shown
The faults of others, not disguised our own,
Say this of us, we merely stand and quote
The words and sentiments the author wrote,

And he but drew with undiscerning art
What laughter taught him, we but learnt the part.
If he has failed, acquit him of ill-will
And say in charity, he copied ill,
He reproduced the shadow, drew the shade
And blindly copied faults false nature made.
So for indulgence on his faults we pray
We stand converted, and so end our play.

Legend: A Sequel to
Twelve Years On

[The poem was sent to Dudley Carew with a letter, *Catalogue,*
E22, dated "VI Jd Mart. MCMXXII." (Mark Amory reprints part
of the letter. I quote from parts omitted from *Letters*, p. 8. See
Catalogue, E31.) Waugh notes that the poem

was written in a little less than an hour and as you will see is full of
imperfections. I particularly condemn the lines in the first verse
from "the owner" to "the same." However take it for what it is
worth. To your dull wits let me explain that the "allusions["] are
to yourself, Molson, myself, Flynn, Boothby, Bevan & Fulford.
With time, I may bring in Fremlin and some others. As it is you
ask speed.

Text: Manuscript in the Humanities Research Center, *Catalogue*, B11 (misdated 1921 for 1922).]

As you will see the form is in one place at least irregular. I can only
plead speed. [Written on Oxford Union Society stationery.]

> And as the man of thirty went his way
> Perplexed by memory, the Grubber bell—
> —I quote herald of the passing day—
> Sang out the ancient song of Philomel;
> Brief liberty & short enduring ease.
> The owner of the study left his game
> With well contented heart and bloody knees
> To seek those joys which ever stay the same.
> While Art & Literature & Science tire
> Still stands the sacrament of steam & fire.
> And after tea till Chapel life was good
> And talk grew sleepier.
>   "I wish I knew
> All that this pitt could tell us if it would.

I wonder whose it was in '22."
"A man called Carey I've heard people say
Awfully wicked." "Quite a bruisers jaw
Far the most brilliant fellow of his day."
"He used to run a club to rag the corps
For men who hated life."
        "They say he talked
Absurdly and said 'Eugh' with every word."
["]They say he was so stout that when he walked
The chapel shook and when he sang, they heard
The awful sound in Shoreham." "He had met
And loved each Duke & Duchess in deBrett
Of wealth incalculable."
        "And they say
He loved that ugly nephew of the Head
When he was quite a boy — but in his day
Woodard was only tutor." So they said,
And many things beside and all the while
The walls stood still and heard them as they spoke
But when they went to pray a weary smile
Over its grimly plastered features broke.
Where is there wisdom to be found — in Youth?
Ask the dumb plaster — Silence tells the Truth.

Part Three   The Oxford Years

[This was apparently Waugh's first publication at Oxford, of which he wrote to Tom Driberg, "One loses all ambition to be an intellectual. I am reduced to writing light verse for the *Isis* and taking politics seriously" (*Letters*, p. 10). Waugh wrote to Dudley Carew (*Catalogue*, E37; not in *Letters*) that he had amended his life so as not to lose his scholarship on "history previous," a preliminary examination required as an early demonstration of competence. Judging from a subsequent letter to Driberg, the reading for that examination was virtually the only work he did that term (*Letters*, p. 9). Text: *Isis*, May 17, 1922, incorporating holograph emendations made on the copy in Waugh's scrapbook in the Humanities Research Center.]

In St. Simon's Memoirs.

Since first my infant taste was freed
From what I might and might not read,
I've seen some pretty third-rate stuff,
But these, I said, should be enough;
I'ld never read "Tim's West End Notes"
About the shade and cut of coats,
Or offer to my reeling sense
"Society intelligence."
Thus in my self-respecting day
I trod upon the sober way,
And shunned — a snobbish man, but free —
This Tooting Beck vulgarity;
But Oxford rules the taste of Centuries;
Oxford ordains. We hear her on our knees.
So, Duke, I learn your tales of Court and Queen,
And say "This Oxford loves — and Golder's Green."

Evelyn Waugh, Apprentice

*Inscription in a copy of J. S. Mill's "Principles of
Political Economy."*

O Mr. Mill!
Be still! Be still!
Prove what you will.
I've read my fill.
You make me ill,
John Stuart Mill.

Inscription in Rousseau "Contrat Social."

Was this the book which built the guillotine,
Maddened a continent and slew a Queen?
This self-assured insipid pedantry, —
Was this the book which made a nation free.

What have we gained since then? The tumbril's roar
Merges into a deep untroubled snore
Ten times more terrible. I may not sleep,
I must embrace this cataleptic sheep
And tend with faltering French and small desire
This academic rebel's pent out-fire.

Would I were shipwrecked on some coral shore
Where print and paper never reached me more,
I'd gladly live a literary Crusoe,
Devoid of books, if so devoid of Rousseau.

A University Sermon
to Idealists Who
Are Serious Minded
and Intelligent

[Waugh did not comment on this poem in any of the *Letters*, but it is obviously an apologia for his academic sloth. "Scaramel" was the pseudonym Waugh used for much of his Oxford journalism. Text: *Cherwell*, June 8, 1922, p. 66.]

Oh, fierce young men! with flashing eyes,
Ill tailored and unworldly wise,
Who pace conversant up and down,
Most scholarly in flowing gown,
Using great words with pond'rous ease.
Oh, Errant Knights with bagging knees!
Oh, brave young men, so sure of right,
Be gracious you who shine so bright,
And do not scorn us fools, whose sight
Is blinded by such wealth of light.
We do not wish, we men of dust
To bear more burdens than we must,
We leave the clouds for you to bear
And earth is heavier than air—
Yours the stars and yours the sky,
Why look down so scornfully?
Life is long enough for me,
You may have eternity.
Go on, resplendent men of fire;
Eventually you may tire,
And see, perhaps, like clowns below
That things were like this long ago,
And shall be yet for all we know.
Fierce young men! Why worry so?

Centuries ago and more
Oxford heard all this before;

Evelyn Waugh, Apprentice

This the wisdom that the years
Whisper as they melt in tears;
That there's beauty to be found
And great wisdom, on the ground.
Clouds are only mist, but here
Towers and domes stand straight and clear.
For Oxford men should live and die
To seek the Broad and shun the High.

SCARAMEL.

29

Portrait of Young Man With Career

[Waugh's attitude toward Oxford careerists lasted at least until he completed the portrait of Charles Ryder's Cousin Jasper in *Brideshead Revisited*. Text: *Isis*, May 30, 1923, p.xxii.]

Jeremy came into my room at half-past six, just as I was assembling my sponge and towels and dressing gown and things for a bath. I saw him as I came out of my bedroom, looking for something to write a message on. He was making straight for my portfolio of drawing paper. I called and made myself known to him.

Jeremy was in my house at school; he has what would be known in North Oxford as "personality." That is to say he is rather stupid, thoroughly well satisfied with himself, and acutely ambitious. Jeremy purposes to be President of the Union.

I said to him, "Hullo, Jeremy, I am afraid you find me on the point of going to have a bath. I never miss a bath before dinner; I shall to-night if I do not go at once. The bathroom is shut at seven. But do stay and drink some sherry wont you?"

"Thanks," said Jeremy, and sat down.

I reached for the decanter and found it empty. There must have been nearly a bottle there that morning.

"Jeremy, that damned man of mine has finished the sherry. I am sorry."

"Never mind. I'll just smoke a cigarette and go."

My cigarettes are particularly large and take at least a quarter of an hour to smoke. I banished all my dreams of white tiles and steam and took a cigarette myself.

"I haven't anything particular to say," said Jeremy, "I was just passing your College and thought I might as well drop in for a little. It is hard to know what to do before hall, isn't it?"

"I generally have a bath."

"Ah, our baths are not open at this hour."

He propped his feet on the side of the fireplace. He was wearing that detestable sort of dark brown suede shoes that always looks wet.

"Oh, I know one thing I wanted to ask you. I want to meet Richard Pares. I feel he is a man to know."

"An amiable rogue."

"Well, will you introduce me to him."

"You know, I hardly know him."

It was quite true and, besides, I dislike introducing Jeremy to people; as a rule he begins by calling them by their Christian names.

"Nonsense, I'm always seeing you about together. I am not doing anything 'fore lunch on Tuesday. How about then? Or Friday I could manage, but I should prefer Tuesday."

So it was arranged.

There was a pause; I looked at my watch; Jeremy took no notice; I looked again.

"What is the time," he said, "Twenty-three to. Oh, good!—hours yet."

"Before a fools opinion of himself the gods are silent—aye and envious too," I thought.

"I'm speaking 'on the paper' on Thursday."

"Good."

"About the Near East. Macedonia. Oil, you know."

"Ah."

"I think it ought to be rather a good speech."

"Yes."

"Evelyn, you aren't listening; now seriously, what do you really think is wrong with my speaking. What I feel about the Union myself is...."

A blind fury, a mist of fire. We struggled together on the carpet. He was surprisingly weak for his size. The first blow with the poker he dodged and took on his shoulder; the second and third caved his forehead in. I stood up, quivering, filled with a beastly curiosity to find what *was* inside his broken skull. Instead I restrained myself and put his handkerchief over his face.

Outside the door I met my scout. I forgot the sherry.

"Hunt"—I almost clung to him. "There is a gentleman in the room lying on the carpet."

"Yes sir. Drunk, sir?"

I remembered the sherry. "No, as a matter of fact he's dead."

"Dead, sir?"

"Yes, I killed him."

"You don't say so, sir!"

"But Hunt, what are we to do about it?"

"Well, sir, if he's dead, there doesn't seem to be much we can do, does there? Now I remember a gentleman on this staircase once, who killed himself. Poison. It must have been '93 I should think, or '94. A nice quiet gentleman, too, when he was sober. I remember he said to me...."

The voice droned on, "...I liked your speech, but I thought it was 'a little heavy.' What do you think Bagnall meant by that?"

It was the voice of Jeremy. My head cleared. We were still there on opposite sides of the fire. He was still talking.

"...Scaife said...."

At seven o'clock Jeremy rose. "Well, I mustn't keep you from your bath. Don't forget about asking Richard to lunch on Tuesday, will you? Oh, and Evelyn, if you know the man who reports the Union for the *Isis*, you might ask him to give me a decent notice this time."

I try to think that one day I shall be proud of having known Jeremy. Till then....

SCARAMEL.

30

*Antony, Who
Sought Things
That Were Lost*

[This story, Waugh said in *A Little Learning* (p. 189), was influenced by James Branch Cabell's *Jurgen*. Text: *Oxford Broom* 1, no. 3 (June, 1923): 14–20.]

Revolution came late to St. Romeiro and suddenly, Cazarin, the journalist who had been educated in Paris, was said to have proclaimed it. Messengers came to him with the news that students at Vienna had driven out Prince Metternich and perhaps had murdered him; that all Lombardy was in revolt, that the Pope had fled and all his cardinals. And from the coast the fishermen brought other tales, of how the foreigners were torturing men and women at Venice and of things that were done in Naples; how when the Pope left Rome the pillars of St. Peter's were shaken and many of the peasants affirmed that it was the Emperor Napoleon who had done these things, not knowing that he was dead.

Thus and thus revolution came to St. Romeiro and Cazarin and the people came out in the heat of the day and cried before the Duke's palace; Cazarin crying for liberty and the people for the removal of the duty on olives. Then the news came that the Duke had fled and with him all his family. So the people broke down the iron gates which the Duke's grandfather had brought from Milan and burst into the Palace. And they found only a very few, very young soldiers, and since these seemed ill inclined to resist, they killed them; and then feeling much enraged at their own valour, they sought what further they might do. And they cried, "To the Castle!" for there were the prisoners kept and each had some near relative who for some crime or foolishness was imprisoned.

And Cazarin remembered the Count Antony who had been shut up with his lady in the Castle ten years ago. But when the prison was broken open, they found many debtors and thieves and a poor mad woman who had thought herself to be the Queen of Heaven, but of the Count Antony they found nothing, nor of his lady.

Now this is the story of Antony, called by his friends, "Antony, who sought things that were lost." Cazarin, who had been educated at Paris, learned it, in part from what he himself knew and in part from what the turnkey told him.

He was a tall man, this Count Antony, and very beautiful and he was born of a proud family. His fathers had been great men in Italy and had fought with the Spaniards against the French and had their origin, it was said, from no less a person than a Pope himself. And Count Antony had the estates of his fathers and their beauty, but there was that in the heart of Antony which none of his fathers had known. And for this cause Antony's friends called him, "Antony, who sought things that were lost," because he seemed always to be seeking in the future for what had gone before.

And Antony was betrothed to the Lady Elizabeth who was fair and gentle, and with his sad, wondering eyes he would watch her, for she moved graciously; and in the eyes of both of them was love greater than the fathers of Antony had known.

But there were whisperings at St. Romeiro at this time; behind high shutters men would sit long over their wine and talk of "Freedom" and "Unity" and many foolish words; and they would swear oaths together round the table and sign papers, being very young and somewhat kindled with wine. And these things seemed noble to the Count Antony.

But whisperings were too loud and echoed in the Palace; and thus it was that one day, as he returned from visiting the Lady Elizabeth, he found men of the ducal guard waiting before his house; and they took him to the Castle. Then the Lady Elizabeth, full of love for him, cried to the Duke and prayed for Antony. And when her prayers for his liberty were of no avail she prayed that she might be locked up with him, for, she said, there would be no captivity where Antony was and no freedom where he was not; for she was still a maid and very full of love. And the Duke who, albeit a great lover in his time, was now sunken into a life of gluttony, was afraid of the love in the Lady Elizabeth's eyes and so granted her wish; thus she was borne to the Castle, rejoicing.

These things Cazarin had seen with his own eyes before he went to Paris; what followed after to Antony and Elizabeth he learned from the turnkey, a lame and ugly man, before he was killed by the people of St. Romeiro.

They shut Antony and Elizabeth in a cell cut deeply in the grey stone; it was a dark place and water dripped monotonously from the damp roof to the damp floor and foul things crept about the damp walls. At the side of the cell furthest from the door was a broad step raised from the floor and covered with straw. And there the Lady Elizabeth sat and when the turnkey brought them their food, Antony knelt by her and served her. And after they had eaten thus, they wrapped their hands in each others and talked; and as they talked, they kissed. And they made a bed of straw on the step and thus among the foul and creeping things was their marriage made; and the turnkey envied them that were so happy in so foul a place.

So a week wore itself out and another; and the cheeks of the Lady Elizabeth became pale and her hair became dull and coarse and the brows of the Count Antony that had been white, were dirty and his beard was long; but ever in his smouldering eyes there was love and a seeking for things that were lost. But the turnkey, who had so envied them, saw that now there was in the eyes of the lady Elizabeth no love but only a great weariness.

Now when the turnkey brought them their food, Antony knelt to serve his lover as he had done before. And some of the bread which the turnkey brought was rotten and the lady Elizabeth would tear out what was good with her dirty hands and eat it, and then sullenly roll herself over on the straw and stare at the wall; and Antony would eat what the lady Elizabeth left. And after a short time these two, who had so loved each other, slept together in the straw no longer, but Antony slept on the wet stone; and by day they talked little to each other and never kissed; and the turnkey saw that in the eyes of Antony there was a wild and bewildered sorrow and a seeking for what was no more; but in the eyes of his lover there grew hate.

So autumn grew into winter and a new year began. And the turnkey was lame and his face was scarred with pox and his mouth was drawn with laughing at the sorrow about him; and daily he came to the cell and no other man did the lady Elizabeth see, except Antony who had been her lover. And as winter grew into spring and the hate increased in the eyes of Elizabeth, so there grew also desire for the love of that man that was lost to her. And Antony who slept on the wet stones and ate the rotten bread was agued and sick and too weak to move from his corner; only his eyes followed Elizabeth as she moved in the cell.

One day when the food had been set before her, the lady Elizabeth said, "Turnkey, am I still beautiful?"

And the turnkey answered:

"Not with the beauty in which I first saw you, Lady Elizabeth; for your cheeks are grown pale and your hair dull and coarse, and all your fair skin is blotched and dirty. Yet are you still very beautiful."

"I have not seen my image for many months. Let me look in your eyes and see if I am still beautiful."

So the turnkey thrust his face which was pock-marked and drawn with derision near the face of the Lady Elizabeth; and there was desire in their eyes. And she put her hands in his hair and she leaned her breast against his and so the Lady Elizabeth, who had known the white arms of Antony, loved this turnkey who was ugly and low born. And Antony made no sound but lay in his corner burdened with his ague and the great chain which he could barely move; but in his eyes there was pain as is seldom seen in men.

And the turnkey said, "I will go and bring wine and we will make a feast for this new love which we have found." And they spoke of this new thing which had come to them, and how they would entertain it; and the turnkey promised that she should leave the cell and live with him in his lodgings, where there should be water for her to wash herself and clean food for her to eat and a small courtyard to walk in, whence could be seen the tops of trees. And she cried, "O my love, return to me soon."

Thus was she left with Antony.

And Antony was weak and burdened with his chain but there was pain in him which raised him from his corner; and he spoke no word but crept to Elizabeth, who had been his lover, silently, as the foul things on the walls. And she rose in alarm and made to escape him, but he caught at her ankle and drew her to the floor. And between his hands was the heavy chain and he stretched it across her throat and knelt on the two ends between his wrists so that the great links pressed into her neck. And Elizabeth, who had been his lover, struggled with him, but the pain lent him strength and he prevailed; and the struggling of her hands ceased and thus the lady Elizabeth died.

And so the turnkey found them when he returned; and he uttered a cry and the flask of wine slipped from his fingers and scattered itself on the wet floor. And he ran to where the Lady Elizabeth lay and laid his hand on her breast and knew that she was dead. And spoke no word but left her with Antony and shut the great door and locked it and threw the key into the Castle moat. And he never returned to the cell to tend the body of Elizabeth, for he had known love there.

These things he told Cazarin, who had been educated at Paris, before the people of St. Romeiro killed him.

31

Edward of Unique Achievement

[This is probably the story "in which an earnest student might find hints of my first novel" (*A Little Learning*, p. 189), though the resemblances are confined to aristocratic audacity and a death glossed over with the aid of a drunken doctor. Text: *Cherwell*, August 1, 1923, pp. 14, 16–18.]

I have for a long time hesitated to tell this story of Edward. For six weeks past, since Edward late one evening interrupted my essay to grow expansive over my whisky, I have done the manly thing and told no one—at least practically no one. But lately this wasting of "copy"—as all good journalists are wont to describe the misfortunes of their friends—has been for me a matter of increasing and intolerable regret; and now that I have learned from Anne "in a manner which it is not convenient to record," much of which Edward and Poxe are ignorant, I find it wholly impossible to remain silent. I have obscured the identities of the chief actors so far as it has been in my power to do so. Edward at any rate I feel should be safe from detection.

The more I consider the nature of Edward the more incredible it all seems. He is to all outward showing the most wholly and overmasteringly ordinary undergraduate. Every afternoon, nearly, he may be heard ordering his tea down the Carlton Club telephone, "China tea, dry toast and butter and white cake, for one, please." He is clothed in tweeds or flannels and usually wears an old Wykamist tie. No proctor would hesitate to recognise him as a member of the University.

Yet in this is Edward alone among all the other young men in old Wykamist ties and the Carlton Club. Some few weeks ago he murdered his tutor, a Mr. Curtis. So very few people out of College were aware of Mr. Curtis' existence that his sudden death was received without consternation. He was just no more seen, as un-distinguished dons do disappear in large Colleges. After all it was to everyone's interest to keep things quiet — Mr. Curtis' sole relative, a brother with a large practice at Pangbourne, quite realised this when the Warden explained things to him. The police, I think, never heard of it; if they did it was quite soon forgotten. It was said by Poxe — though with how much truth I would not venture to judge — that pressure was brought on Collingridge to keep the affair out of the *Isis* (There was some doubt about his degree — the Dean of Edwards' College was examining it — but, as I say, I will not make myself responsible for anything Poxe says).

I do not know why Edward hated Mr. Curtis so much. I never had the privilege of meeting him but as I used to watch him moving about, the quad usually alone or with Anne, who is married to the Warden, I thought that he seemed, considering that he was a history tutor, a pleasant young man enough. But, however that may be, Edward hated him with an absorbing and unmeasurable hatred, so that at last he became convinced that Mr. Curtis' existence was not compatible with his own. This was a state of mind into which any undergraduate might have slipped; where Edward showed himself essentially different from the other young men in Old Wykamist ties in the Carlton Club, was in his immediate perception that the more convenient solution was not suicide but murder. Most undergraduates would kill themselves sooner or later if they stayed up long enough, very few would kill anyone else.

Once decided upon, the murder was accomplished with the straight-forward efficiency which one would expect from a student of the cinematograph and one who, until his second failure in History previous (through his inability to draw maps) had been a senior History scholar.

Mr. Curtis' room was on the first floor just above the side gate. The side gate was closed at nine and the key kept in the porter's lodge. The other key was kept in the Bursary. Edward knew that this was the key which he would have to take. He went into the Bursary at lunch time and found the Bursar there. The keys were hung on a nail by his desk. The Bursar sat at the desk. Edward began a story of a burned carpet; the Bursar became angry but did not move. He included the sofa; the Bursar stood up but remained at his desk. Edward threw a chair into the conflagration and then described how the three minimax extinguishers which he had promised were all empty, "perhaps during the Bump supper, you know, sir." It was enough; the Bursar strode up and down thoroughly moved; Edward secured the key and hurrying to his room burned the carpet and the sofa and the chair and emptied the extinguishers in case the Bursar should come to investigate. His scout thought him drunk.

Edward then hurried to Mr. Curtis and secured an interview for ten that evening; he sent a note to the President of the Union desiring to speak that evening, it was on Thursday that these things occurred — and then feeling that he had accomplished a good work, lunched very quietly at the Carlton Club.

After lunch Edward set out on his bicycle and rode through much dust to Abingdon. There not at the first antique shop but at the smaller one on the other side of the square, he bought a dagger; at Radley he bought a stone and sitting under a hedge he sharpened it. Returning with this in his pocket he lay for a long time in a very hot bath. It was with considerable contentment that he sat down to eat dinner alone at the George — there were still several details to be thought out.

The Union that evening was fuller than usual; some politician from London of enormous distinction was speaking. Edward, in private business, asked questions of force and ingenuity about the despatch boxes, the clock, the gas burners in the roof, and the busts of the Prime Ministers, he was observed by all. At five to ten he slipped out saying to the Teller as he went that he was coming back; others were about him who were making for the coffee room while drinks could still be obtained. Edward's bicycle was among the others at the St. Michael Street gate, clustering about the notice which forbade their presence. In eight minutes he was back again in his place, reviewing with complete satisfaction his evening's achievement; almost immediately he was called upon to speak. His speech was, perhaps, more successful as an alibi than as a piece of oratory, but few were there to hear it. As he walked home that evening there was singing in his heart. It had been an admirable murder. Everything had happened perfectly. He had gone in at the side gate, unobserved, and reached Mr. Curtis' room. His tutor had that habit, more fitting for a house master than a don, of continuing to read or write some few words after his visitors entered, in order to emphasize his superiority. It was while he was finishing his sentence that Edward killed him and the sentence was merged into a pool of blood. On his way back, Edward had gone down George Street as far as the canal and there had sunk the dagger. It had been a good evening, Edward thought.

Hastings, the night porter at Edwards' College, always liked to delay people and talk to them in the porch. It was a habit which many resented, but Edward tonight was so overflowing with good nature that he actually started the conversation.

"A dull debate at the Union to-night, Hastings."

"Indeed, sir; and did you speak."?

"I tried to."

"Ah, well sir; if you wanted excitement you should have stayed in College to-night. Most unusual happenings, sir. I don't think I ever remember anything quite like it happening before, not since I've been at the College."

"Why, what's happened Hastings?"

"You may well ask sir. I knew his Lordship would come to a bad end."

"Do tell me what has happened, Hastings."

"Well, sir, you knows what Lord Poxe is when he gets drunk, sir. There's no stopping him. Well, he come in to-night, sir, oh very drunk. He never see me when I opened the door — just ran straight in and fell down on the grass. Then he gets up and starts swearing something wicked — said the dons hadn't no right to put grass there for a gentleman to fall over. Said he was going to go and murder the lot of them."

"Well, Hastings."

"Well, he's done it, sir."

"What! all of them, Hastings?"

"No, sir, not all; but Mr. Curtis, sir. The Dean went to find him to tell him to go to bed and found him asleep on the floor of Mr. Curtis' room and Mr. Curtis," with great glee, "dripping blood, sir. Quite slowly, pit-a-pat, as you might say."

"Well, I'm damned."

"Yes, indeed, sir. So was the Dean. He is with the Warden now, sir."

The sky filled with chimes; it was twelve o'clock.

"Well, I must go to bed Hastings. It's a funny business."

"Yes, sir, and good night sir."

"Good night Hastings."

So Edward went to bed with a grave disquiet. It was a pity that Poxe should have done this; it was really a very great pity. But as he grew sleepier the conviction grew that perhaps this was the best that could happened. He thought of Poxe — a sad figure. His father had been forced to resign from the Diplomatic Corps after that disgraceful business with the Montenegran ministers' younger daughter, and had then marked his first cousin, begotten an heir and drunken himself to death at the age of forty-two. It was thought that Poxe would never beget an heir, and it was certain that he would not live to be forty-two. He was nearly always half-sober. And so Edward's thoughts drifted to the decay of great families, to renaissance Italy, and then far away beyond St. Mary's tower where it was just striking half-past twelve. A good evening and sleep. . . .

Everyone in College had heard the story next morning. It reached me through my scout who called me with: "Half-past seven, sir, and Lord Poxe has murdered Mr. Curtis." I met Poxe in the bathroom, very white and dejected. I asked him about the murder.

"Well, I suppose I've rather rotted things up this time. I can't remember a thing about it except that I was furious about some grass, and that two people put me to bed. It's a melancholy business. They can't hang me, can they?"

I suggested inebriates' asylum and had my bath. I was sincerely sorry about poor Poxe, but felt he would probably be better shut up. After all it was not safe to have a man who did that sort of thing, about the College; it was not as though he was seldom drunk. I went to breakfast at the Old Oak tea rooms and found Edward there. He was in great form, and for this I disliked him that he should be in good form at breakfast; however, he was really rather amusing about the Poxe murder, as it was already called.

Edward asked if he might work in my rooms — he knew I never used them — as he had had a fire in his. I said that I wanted them this morning and advised the Union. Then I went back.

At about eleven, I saw from my window the Warden's side door open and Poxe come out, radiantly cheerful. I called him into my room, and he told me of what had happened. It must certainly have been a cheering interview for Poxe.

He had gone to see the Warden with all the trepidation that should befit a young nobleman suddenly confronted with the prospect of being hanged. The old man had been seated on one side of the table with the Dean next to him. Poxe had been asked to sit down. The warden had began:

"I have asked you to come and see me, Lord Poxe, in what for both of us I think, and certainly for me, is a very bitter occasion. Last night, when in a state of intoxication, as you will perhaps have been informed, you entered the room of your tutor, Mr. Curtis, and stabbed him to death. I suppose that you do not deny this?"

Poxe was silent.

"It was a foolish act, Lord Poxe, an act of wanton foolishness, but I do not wish to be hard on you," the Wardens voice broke with emotion, "my poor boy, you are the fifteenth Lord Poxe and as I have at different occasions reminded you, not unconnected with my own family. Lady Emily Crane, your great aunt, you will remember, married a Mr. Arthur Thorn, my grandfather. I feel that the College owes it to your position to treat this matter as discreetly as possible."

Poxe nodded enthusiastically. Among tradesmen and dons he had always found his title of vast value.

"The Dean and I have discussed the matter at some length and have come to the conclusion that there is no reason why this matter should be referred to the ordinary state authorities at all; it has, as, of course you are aware, always been a principle of University government so far as is possible to impede and nullify the workings of the ordinary courts of law. In this case it seems particularly advisable, as it is only too likely that the criminal courts would be unwilling to treat this matter with the clemency which we think desirable.

"Nor, indeed, is a precedent far to seek. In the fifteenth century a commoner of this college struck off the head of the Bursar—true that was in open fight and not before the young man had received severe injuries; but things, of course, were far rougher then. On that occasion the distinguished scholar, who held the position it is my privilege unworthily to occupy, inflicted upon the delinquent the fine of twopence to be paid to the Bursar's relatives."

Poxe brightened.

"Of course, the value of the penny has, since that time, markedly decreased, but calculating it as nearly as one can in days of rather haphazard accountancy, the Dean and I decided that the fine must have valued about thirteen shillings.

"I need hardly say, Lord Poxe, that this whole matter has been acutely distressing to the Dean and myself. We hope and trust that it will not occur again. It is probable that in the event of a second offence, the College would find itself unable to treat the matter with the same generosity. Thank you, Lord Poxe."

And thus the interview closed and Poxe went out, elated, to celebrate his escape in the manner which most immediately suggested itself to him; and Edward, in his fire-blackened room felt that everything was turning out well.

Without difficulty, an aged and dissolute doctor was unearthed in St. Ebbs, where he lodged in squalor with one of the College servants, and earned an irregular livelihood by performing operations in North Oxford; this sorry man was persuaded to write a certificate of death from natural causes. The funeral was brief and ill-attended. The Warden toiled for three days in the composition of a Greek epitaph and on the third evening persuaded the Dean to write one in Latin. And so for Poxe and Edward the matter ended.

One thing I feel should be added. It is merely an incident that may be of no significance but which may explain much that seems improbable. I was told it, in an intimate moment by Anne, who is married to the Warden and of whom many stories are told. This is what she said, that on the night when Mr. Curtis died, she ran in a high state of emotion to her husband, the Warden, and cried, "Oh why, why did you kill him? I never really loved him?"

She stopped seeing the Dean there also. He, a gentleman, rose to go, but the Warden detained him. And then Anne, falling on her knees, pounded out a tale of the most monstrous and unsuspected transactions between herself and Mr. Curtis.

"Supposing there were a trial," asked the Warden, "could this be kept a secret."

The Dean doubted gravely whether this would be possible.

And then came to the Warden the full realisation of the imperishable obligations of precedent, the memory of the head of the Bursar, the appreciation of the greatness of families not unconnected with his own.

"At least, I think it must have been then," Anne said as she turned up the light. SCARAMEL.

32

[This is the first and most romantic fictional appearance of the
name Imogen. Waugh used it, with decreasing emotion, in "The
Balance" and, as the imaginary Imogen Quest, in *Vile Bodies*.
Text: *Cherwell*, August 15, 1923, p. 42.]

Almost the first thing which Toby said to me when we met was,
"Imogen is in London again."

Even to Toby to whom this could never mean as much as to the
rest of us, it seemed the only thing of immediate importance; to me,
more than as pleasure or pain, though, of course, it was both of
these, it came as a breaking away of near memories.

For some moment of time the bar where we stood was frozen in
space; the handles, the slopped wood, the pallid man beyond them
lost perspective; "If you like our beer tell your friends; if you don't
tell us" stood as cut in stone, the ordainment of priest kings,
immeasurably long ago; the three years or a little more that stood
between now and that grim evening in April fell, unhonoured, into
the remote past and there was no sound from the street.

Then, instantly almost, the machine fell to its work again and I
said as though nothing had intervened between his voice and mine.

"Was she with *him?*"

For even now, after three years or more, I could not easily say his
name; I spoke of him, as slatternly servants will speak of their
master, impersonally. And indeed it was thus I thought of him; the
name was an insignificant thing labelling an event. Toby understood something of this as anyone who had known Imogen, must
have understood, even he; for he was associated with much that was
wholly alien to him; he had been in Adelphi Terrace in that strange
evening in April when Hauban had gazed out across the river for
two, three hours, and scarely a word spoken.

To my question, down such valleys of thought, his answer made a way; she had been with him; they in a taxi; Toby had seen it from the top of a 'bus in Regent Street.

And so, quite naturally, I went to find Hauban, whom I had not thought to seek when I had landed that morning — or was it three and a half years ago? Thus suddenly had I returned to the past. And when I found Hauban, he said.

"So you, also, are returned to England."

Thus I knew that he too had seen Imogen and with his next words he invited me to dinner where I should meet many old friends, whom he would assemble to greet my return. But he and I and his guests knew that not for my welcome were we assembled, though no word was spoken of Imogen all the evening through.

And the thought of her was about and between us all; with such shy courtesy did we treat her, who had been Queen, for all who had loved her were gathered there and none dared speak even her name.

SCARAMEL.

33

Conspiracy to Murder

[Waugh was frequently macabre, but this is his only excursion into the horrible ("Unacademic Exercise" might have been another had it been published in completed form). However, he used the figure of the mysterious stranger — the man who dines at a separate table aboard the *S.S. Caliban* — in *The Ordeal of Gilbert Pinfold*. Text: *Cherwell*, September 5, 1923, pp. 116, 118.]

During the first week of term, Guy first mentioned his neighbour to me. We were sitting on my window seat looking over the quad, when I noticed slinking out of the J.C.R. a strange shambling man of middle age. He was ill-dressed and rather dirty, and he peered forward as he walked.

"That strange man," said Guy, "has got the room opposite me."

We decided that this would be dull for Guy, for we had often seen these strange old men before and knew that they had no interest to offer, except the dull curiosity of asking why they had come to Oxford. And they were nearly always ready to tell their story of miserly saving and the thirst for knowledge. Therefore when, a fortnight later, Guy began to talk of him again, I was considerably surprised.

"You know, he leads an incredible life; my scout told me that he has never been out to a meal or had a single man in to see him. He doesn't know one of the other freshers and can't find his way about Oxford. He's never heard of half the Colleges. I think I shall go in and talk to him one evening. Come up with me."

So one evening at about half-past ten, Guy and I went across to this strange man's room. We knocked, and getting no answer, opened the door. The room was in darkness, and we were about to go, when Guy said: "Let's have a look at his room."

I turned on his light and then gave a gasp of astonishment. The little man was sitting in his arm chair with his hands in his lap looking straight at us. We began to apologise, but he interrupted us.

"What do you want? I do not wish to be disturbed."

"Our names are Guy Legge and Barnes." I said, "we just came in to see you, but if you're busy—" I was strangely discomforted by this man and had not yet recovered from the shock of finding him sitting there in the dark.

"It was unnecessary to come and see me. I don't want to know you Barnes, or you Legge, or anyone else."

And outside the door I said, "Well I'm damned. Of all the abominable men—"

But Guy took me by the arm and said, "Dick, that man scared me."

So it began.

A few nights later I was engrossed in an essay when I heard someone beating on my oak.

"Go away, I'm busy."

"It's I, Guy. May I come in?"

"Oh, it's you. Well do you mind awfully if I work to-night. I've got to get this essay done by eleven to-morrow."

"Let me in, Dick. I won't disturb you. I only wanted to know if I could come in and read in here."

So I opened the oak and when he came into the light I saw that he was looking pale and worried.

"Thanks awfully, Dick. I hope you don't mind my coming in. I couldn't work in my room."

So I returned to my essay and in two hours it was finished. I turned round and saw that Guy was not working. He was just sitting gazing into my fire.

"Well," I said, "I've finished this thing and I'm going to bed."

He roused himself, "Well, I suppose I must get back," and then at the door, "You know, Dick, that man next door haunts me. I've never met a man who hated me as he does. When we meet on the stairs, he shrinks away and snarls like a beast."

And I, sleepily, laughed at him and went to bed.

And for the next week or so, Guy came to my room every evening until one Sunday night he said, "Dick, I don't want to go back, I'm not sleepy. May I read in front of your fire all night."

I told him not to be a fool; he was looking thoroughly tired. And then he said, "Dick, don't you understand, I'm afraid of that man next door. He wants to kill me."

"Guy," I said, "go to bed and don't be an ass. You have been working too hard."

But a quarter of an hour later, I felt that I could not go to bed and leave Guy like this, so I went up to his room. As I passed the strange man's door, I could not help a little qualm of fear. I knocked at Guy's bedroom door and inside I heard a little cry of terror and the sound of bare feet. I turned the handle, but the door was locked and I could hear Guy's breathing through the door; he must have been pressed against it on the other side.

"D'you always lock your bedder door?" I asked, and at the sound of my voice I heard him sigh with relief.

"Hullo, Dick. You quite startled me. What do you want?"

So I went in and talked to him; he always slept with his door locked now, and his light on; he was very much scared but after a few minutes he became calmer and soon I went away, but behind me I heard him lock his door.

Next day he avoided me until evening; then he came in again and asked if he might work. I said:

"Look here, Guy, tell me what is the matter with you." And almost immediately I wished that I had not asked him, because he poured out his answers so eagerly.

"Dick, you can't think what I've been through in the last ten days. I'm living up there along with only a door between me and a madman. He hates me, Dick, I know it. It is not imagination. Every night he comes and tries at my door and then shuffles off again. I can't stand it. One night I shall forget and then God knows what that man will do to me."

So it went on and one day I went up to Guy's room in the morning. He was not there, but his scout was, and I found him in the act of taking the key from Guy's bedroom door. I knew I had no right to ask him, but I said:

"Hullo, Ramsey, what are you doing with Mr. Legge's key?"

Ramsey showed, as only a scout can show, that I had been guilty of a gross breach of good manners and answered me.

"The gentleman next door wanted it, sir. He has lost his and wanted to see if it would fit."

"Did Mr. Legge say that you could take it?"

"No, sir. I did not think it necessary to ask him."

"Then put it back at once and don't touch things in his room whatever the gentleman next door says."

I had no right to say this to Guy's scout, but I was definitely frightened. A sudden realisation had come to me that Guy might have some reason for his fear. That evening I went up to see him and we decided to work in his room. He did not mind if I were with him.

"But shut the oak, Dick," he said.

We worked until eleven o'clock and then we both sat up listening; someone was fumbling against the oak; then he knocked quietly.

Guy had started up white and panting.

"You see, I haven't been lying. He's coming at me. Keep him off, Dick, for god's sake."

The knocking was repeated.

"Guy," I said, "I'm going to open that oak. Brace up, man, we two can look after ourselves against anyone. Don't you see? We've got to open that oak.

"Dick, for God's sake don't. I can't stand it," but I went towards the door. I opened it and there was only the oak between us and the man beyond. Suddenly Guy's face became twisted with hatred and his voice harsh. "So you're in it, too. You're going to betray me to that fiend. He's bought you as he has bought Ramsey. There's not a man in the College he hasn't bought or bullied into it and I can't fight the lot," his voice suddenly fell to a tone of blind despair and he rushed into his bedroom, slamming the door. I hesitated between the two doors and then, picking up a heavy candlestick, opened the oak.

On the threshold, blinking the light, was the strange man.

"So you're here, too, Barnes," he said slowly; "but that is excellent. What I wish to say is for you as well as Legge. I want to apologise for being so rude that evening when you two came up to see me. I was very nervous. But where is Legge?"

And from the bedroom came a sound of hysterical sobbing, the wild, hideous sobbing of a mad man.

34

Unacademic Exercise:
A Nature Story

[Text: *Cherwell*, September 19, 1923, pp. 152–53. The final sentence was added in Waugh's handwriting on the copy in his scrapbook in the Humanities Research Center.]

After half-an-hour I said what I had been pondering ever since we started.

"Billy, this is a crazy business. I'm willing to call the bet off if you are."

But he answered gravely.

"I'm sorry, my friend, but I'm not going to lose the opportunity of making a fiver."

Then there was silence again until Anderson looked back from the wheel and said:

"Look here, Billy, let's stop at this pub and then go home. I can lend you a fiver or more if you want it. You needn't pay me until you want to."

But Billy was resolute:

"No, Dick, I owe enough already. I should like to earn an honest meal for once."

So Anderson drove on and soon we came into sight of the grim place which Craine had chosen for our experiment. I saw that Billy was beginning to lose his nerve for he was shivering in his big overcoat and his feet were very still, pressed down with all his might.

"Billy," I said, "I don't think we need go any further; we should only be wasting time. You've obviously won the bet."

And I think he would have yielded—for he was rather a child—when Craine's voice answered for him.

"What damned nonsense. The thing isn't begun yet. Donne's bet that he has the nerve to go through the whole werewolf ceremony. Just getting to the place is nothing. He doesn't yet know what he has to do. I've got as far as this twice before—once in Nigeria with a man of forty, but he hadn't the nerve to go through with it, and once in Wales with the bravest thing in the world, a devoted woman; but she couldn't do it. Donne may, because he's young and hasn't seen enough to make him easily frightened."

But Billy was frightened, badly, and so were Anderson and I and for this reason we let ourselves be overborne by Craine because he knew that we were; and he smiled triumphant as a stage Satan in the moonlight.

It was strange being beaten like this by Craine who in College was always regarded as a rather unsavoury joke. But then this whole expedition was strange and Craine was an old man—thirty-three— an age incalculable to the inexperience of twenty-one; and Billy was only just nineteen.

We had started off merrily enough down St. Aldate's, Billy had said:

"I wonder what human flesh tastes like; what d'you suppose one should drink with it?" and when I had answered with utter futility, "Spirits, of course," they had all laughed; which shows that we were in high good humour.

But once in Anderson's car and under that vast moon, a deep unquiet had settled upon us and when Craine said in his sinister way:

"By the way, Donne, you ought to know in case you lose us; if you want to regain your manhood all you have to do is to draw some of your own blood and take off the girdle."

Anderson and I shuddered. He said it with a slight sneer on "manhood" and we resented it that he should speak to Billy in this way, but more than this we were shocked at the way in which the joke was suddenly plunged into reality. This was the first time that evening on which I had felt fear and all through the drive it had grown more and more insistent, until on the heath, bleak and brilliantly moon-lit, I was sickeningly afraid and said:

"Billy, for God's sake let's get back."

But Craine said quietly:

·"Are you ready, Donne? The first thing you have to do is to take off your clothes; yes, all of them."

And Billy without looking at us, began with slightly trembling hands to undress. When he stood, white beside his heap of clothes under the moon, he shivered and said: "I hope I get a wolf skin soon; it's damned cold." But the pathetic little joke faltered and failed and left us all shivering; all except Craine who was pouring something out into the cup of his flask.

"You have to drink this—all right it isn't poisonous. I brewed it myself out of roots and things."

So the rites began. Billy was told to draw a circle about himself in the ground and he obeyed silently. Another potion was given to him.

"Put this on your hands, eye lids, navel and feet. Just a drop or two. That's right."

I was trembling unrestrainedly and I dared not look at Anderson because I knew that he was too. Craine went on evenly:

"And now comes a less pleasant part. I am afraid that you have to taste human blood," and then to us, like a conjuror borrowing a watch, "will either of you two volunteer to lend some?"

Anderson and I started, thoroughly alarmed.

"Look here, Craine, this is beastly."

"You can't go on, Craine."

But Craine said:

"Well, Donne, what are we going to do?" and Billy answered evenly, "Go on with it, Craine."

It was the first time he had spoken since he drew the circle and he stood now quite calm and looking incredibly defenceless.

"Well, if neither of you two friends of his are willing, I suppose I must offer my blood."

But by a sudden intuition, we both of us knew that this thing must be averted at all costs; I was conscious of the most immediate and overpowering danger and dreamlike stood unmoving; Anderson had started forward.

"If Billy wants to go on with this, he had better have mine."

And Craine answered easily:

"As you like, my friend. Do not step inside the circle and cut deeply because he will need a good deal. That is all I ask you," but he and Anderson and I knew that he had been in some strange way checked.

So Anderson rolled up his sleeve and cut his arm and Billy without hesitation put his lips to the wound. After a few moments, Craine said, "That should be enough"; so Anderson bound up his arm roughly with a handkerchief and Billy straightened himself; there was a small trickle of blood running down his chin. He was made to repeat some jumbled sentences in a foreign tongue and then Craine produced a strip of fur.

"The girdle," he said, "put it on Donne."

"And now you have to kneel down and say a paternoster backwards. You had better repeat it after me."

And then there occurred something of which, I think, I shall never lose the memory. Billy did not kneel down; he crouched back on his haunches like an animal and threw his head right back; his fair hair stirred in the moonlight, but on his face there came a look of awakening and of savagery, his lips drawn back and showing his teeth. I stood there in wild horror and saw this happen.

"Amen, Saeculorum Saecula in gloria."

And the Thing in the circle drew in its breath. I dare not now think what that sound might have been. I refuse resolutely to let myself consider the possibility that it might not have been Billy's voice; that the Thing in the circle was not Billy, his face contorted by some trick of the moonlight. Even then, in that moment of terror, I would not let myself consider this but I knew by an animal apprehension of the Unknown that that sound must be stopped if we were to keep our sanity; that from the moment we heard it our lives must be wholly altered. Anderson knew this, too; and, always quicker to act than I, he was in the circle while I stood numb with horror. He was a strong man and he flung Billy across the scratched circumference, tearing the girdle from him; he fell in a heap and his elbow struck on a stone; a drop of blood oozed through the earth. Then he raised himself, and, holding his elbow said, "Dick, are you mad? Why on earth did you do that? You've hurt me damnably."

And then suddenly turning onto his face he burst into a fit of hysterical crying and lay there shaking from head to foot and we three watching him. Craine, of course, spoke first.

The rest omitted owing to blind stupidity of editor and printer.

35

The National Game

[Waugh hated cricket as much as his brother, Alec, loved—and excelled at—the game. Text: *Cherwell*, September 26, 1923, pp. 174, 176.]

My brother said to me at breakfast:

"When you last played cricket, how many runs did you make?" And I answered him, truthfully, "fifty."

I remembered the occasion well for this was what happened. At school, oh! many years ago now, I had had my sixth form privileges taken away for some unpunctuality or other trifling delinquency and the captain of cricket in my house, a youth with whom I had scarcely ever found myself in sympathy, took advantage of my degraduation to put me in charge of a game, called quite appropriately a "Remnants' game." I had resented this distinction grimly, but as a matter of fact the afternoon had been less oppressive than I had expected. Only twenty-one boys arrived so, there being none to oppose me, I elected to play for both while they were batting. I thus ensured my rest and for an hour or so read contentedly having gone in first and failed to survive the first over. When eventually by various means the whole of one side had been dismissed—the umpire was always the next batsman, and, eager for his innings, was usually ready to prove himself sympathetic with the most extravagant appeal.—I buckled on the pair of pads which a new boy had brought, although they were hotly claimed by the wicket keeper, and went out to bat. This other side bowled less well and after missing the ball once or twice, I suddenly and to my intense surprise hit it with great force. Delighted by this I did it again and again. The fielding was half-hearted and runs accumulated. I asked the scorer how many I had made and was told "thirty-six." Now and then I changed the bowlers, being still captain of the fielding side and denounced those who were ostentatiously slack in the field. Soon I saw a restiveness about both sides and much looking of watches. "This game shall not end," I ordained, "until I have made fifty." Almost immediately the cry came "Fifty" and with much clapping I allowed the stumps to be drawn.

Such is the history of my only athletic achievement. On hearing of it my brother said, "Well, you'd better play to-day. Anderson has just fallen through. I'm taking a side down to a village in Hertfordshire — I've forgotten the name."

And I thought of how much I had heard of the glories of village cricket and of that life into which I had never entered and so most adventurously, I accepted.

"Our train leaves King's Cross at 9:20. The taxi will be here in five minutes. You'd better get your things."

At quarter past nine we were at the station and some time before eleven the last of our team arrived. We learned that the village we were to play was called Torbridge. At half-past twelve, we were assembled with many bags on the Torbridge platform. Outside two Fords were for hire and I and the man who had turned up latest succeeded in discovering the drivers in the "Horse and Cart"; they were very largely sober; it seemed that now everything would be going well. My brother said,

"Drive us to the cricket ground."

"There isn't no cricket ground," brutishly, "is there, Bill?"

"I have heard that they do play cricket on Beesley's paddock."

"Noa, that's football they plays there."

"Ah; very craftily, "but that's in the winter. Mebbe they plays cricket there in the summer."

"I have heard that he's got that field for hay this year."

"Why, so 'e 'ave."

"No, there ain't no cricket ground, mister." And then I noticed a sign post. On one limb was written "Lower Torbridge, Great Torbridge, Torbridge St. Swithin," and on the other "Torbridge Heath, South Torbridge, Torbridge Village," and on the third just "Torbridge Station," this pointing towards me.

We tossed up and, contrary to the lot, decided to try Torbridge Village. We stopped at the public house and made enquiries. No, he had not heard of no match here. They did say there was some sort of festification at Torbridge St. Swithin, but maybe that was the flower show. We continued the pilgrimage and at each public house we each had half-a-pint. At last after three-quarters of an hour, we found at the "Pig and Hammer" Torbridge Heath, eleven disconsolate men. They were expecting a team to play them — "the Reverend Mr. Bundles." Would they play against us instead? Another pint all round and the thing was arranged. It was past one; we decided to lunch at once. At quarter to three, very sleepily the opposing side straddled out into the field. At quarter past four, when we paused for tea, the score was thirty-one for seven, of these my brother had made twenty in two overs and had then been caught; I had made one and that ingloriously. I had hit the ball with great force on to my toe from which it had bounced into the middle of the pitch. "Yes, one," cried the tall man at the other end; he wanted the bowling; with great difficulty I limped across; I was glad that the next ball bowled him. One man did all the work for the other side—a short man with very brown forearms and a bristling moustache.

At quarter to five we went out to field and at seven, when very wearily we went back to the pavilion, only one wicket had fallen for 120. The brown-armed man was still in. Even on the occasion of my triumph I had not fielded; this afternoon, still with a crushed toe, I did not do myself credit. After a time it became the habit of the bowler whenever a ball was hit near me, immediately to move me away and put someone else there; and for this I was grateful.

In the shed at the end of the field there was no way of washing. We all had to change in one little room each with his heap of clothes; we all lost socks, studs and even waistcoats; it was all very like school. And finally when we were changed and feeling thoroughly sticky and weary, we learned from the cheery captain with the brown arms that there were no taxis in Torbridge Heath and no telephone to summon one with. It was three miles to Torbridge Station and the last train left at half-past eight. There would be no time for any dinner; we had heavy bags to carry.

One last sorrow came upon us when it would have seemed that all was finished, and just as we were coming into King's Cross I found that somewhere in that turmoil of changing I had lost my return ticket. My poor brother had to pay, I having no money. When he had paid he discovered that he would have no money left for a taxi. We must go back by tube and walk. To travel by tube with a heavy bag is an uneasy business. And when I returned home, I reasoned thus with myself; to-day I have wearied myself utterly; I have seen nothing and no one of any interest; I have suffered discomfort of every sense and in every limb; I have suffered acute pain in my great toe; I have walked several miles; I have stood about for several hours; I have drunken several pints of indifferently good beer; I have spent nearly two pounds; I might have spent that sum in dining very well and going to a theatre; I might have made that sum by spending the morning, pleasantly, in writing or drawing.

But my brother maintained that it had been a great day. Village cricket, he said, was always like that.

SCARAMEL.

Part Four   Becoming a Man of Letters

[Waugh began to work on this story, in which he first attempted to establish an objective point of view, in May, 1925, while he was teaching in Wales and not long after he destroyed what was apparently the rather precious if not whimsical "The Temple at Thatch." For the process of composition, see *Diaries*, pp. 211, 212, 218. Text: *Georgian Stories, 1926*, ed. Alec Waugh (New York: G. P. Putnam's Sons, 1927), pp. 279–323 (also published: London: Chapman and Hall, pp. 253–91).]

A Yarn of the Good Old Days of Broad Trousers and
High Necked Jumpers

Introduction

"Do you know, I don't think I *can* read mine. It's rather unkind."

"Oh, Basil, you must."

"Please, Basil."

This always happened when Basil played paper games.

"No, I can't, look it's all scrumbled up."

"Oh, Basil, dearest, do.".

"Oh, Basil, *please*."

"Darling Basil, you must."

"No, I won't. Imogen will be in a rage with me."

"No, she won't, will you, Imogen?"

"Imogen, tell him you won't be in a rage with him."

"Basil, *do* read it please."

"Well, then, if you promise you won't hate me"—and he smoothed out the piece of paper.

"Flower—Cactus.

"Drink—Rum.

"Stuff—Baize.

"Furniture—Rocking-Horse.

"Food—Venison.

"Address—Dublin.

"And Animal—Boa constrictor."

"Oh, Basil, how marvellous."

"Poor Adam, I never thought of him as Dublin, of course it's perfect."

"Why Cactus?"

"So phallic, my dear, and prickly."

"And such vulgar flowers."

"Boa constrictor is brilliant."

"Yes, his digestion you know."

"And can't sting, only crush."

"And fascinates rabbits."

"I must draw a picture of Adam fascinating a rabbit," and then, "Imogen, you're not going?"

"I must. I'm terribly sleepy. Don't get drunk and wake me up, will you?"

"Imogen, you *are* in a rage with me."

"My dear, I'm far too tired to be in a rage with anybody. Good night."

The door shut.

"My dear, she's furious."

"I knew she would be, you shouldn't have made me read it."

"She's been very odd all the evening, I consider."

"She told me she lunched with Adam before she came down."

"I expect she ate too much. One does with Adam, don't you find?"

"Just libido."

"But you know, I'm rather proud of that character all the same. I wonder why none of us ever thought of Dublin before."

"Basil do you think Imogen *can* have been having an *affaire* with Adam, really?"

Circumstances

NOTE. — No attempt, beyond the omission of some of the aspirates, has been made at a phonetic rendering of the speech of Gladys and Ada; they are the cook and house-parlourmaid from a small house in Earls Court, and it is to be supposed that they speak as such.

The conversations in the film are deduced by the experienced picture-goer from the gestures of the actors; only those parts which appear in capitals are actual "captions."

THE COCKATRICE CLUB 2.30 A.M.
A CENTRE OF LONDON NIGHT LIFE

The "Art title" shows a still life of a champagne bottle, glasses, and a comic mask—or is it yawning?

"Oh, Gladys, it's begun; I knew we'd be late."

"Never mind, dear, I can see the way. Oh, I say—I am sorry. Thought the seat was empty—really I did."

Erotic giggling and a slight struggle.

"Give over, can't you, and let me get by—saucy kid."

"'Ere you are, Gladys, there's two seats 'ere."

"Well I never—tried to make me sit on 'is knee."

"Go on. I say, Gladys, what sort of picture is this—is it comic?"

The screen is almost completely dark as though the film has been greatly over-exposed. Fitful but brilliant illumination reveals a large crowd dancing, talking and eating.

"No, Ada—that's lightning. I dare say it's a desert storm. I see a picture like that the other day with Fred."

EVERYBODY LOVES MY BABY

Close up: the head of a girl.

"That's 'is baby. See if she ain't."

It is rather a lovely head, shingled and superbly poised on its neck. One is just beginning to appreciate its exquisite modelling—the film is too poor to give any clear impression of texture—when it is flashed away and its place taken by a stout and elderly man playing a saxophone. The film becomes obscure—after the manner of the more modern Continental studios: the saxophonist has become the vortex of movement; faces flash out and disappear again; fragmentary captions will not wait until they are read.

"Well, I do call this soft."

A voice with a Cambridge accent from the more expensive seats says, "Expressionismus."

Gladys nudges Ada and says, "Foreigner."

After several shiftings of perspective, the focus becomes suddenly and stereoscopically clear. The girl is seated at a table leaning towards a young man who is lighting her cigarette for her. Three or four others join them at the table and sit down. They are all in evening dress.

"No, it isn't comic, Ada—it's Society."

"Society's sometimes comic. You see."

The girl is protesting that she must go.

"Adam, I must. Mother thinks I went out to a theatre with you and your mother. I don't know what will happen if she finds I'm not in."

There is a general leave-taking and paying of bills.

"I say, Gladys, 'e's 'ad a drop too much, ain't 'e?"

The hero and heroine drive away in a taxi.

Half-way down Pont Street, the heroine stops the taxi.

"Don't let him come any farther, Adam. Lady R. will hear."

"Good night, Imogen dear."

"Good night, Adam."

She hesitates for a moment and then kisses him.

Adam and the taxi drive away.

Close up of Adam. He is a young man of about twenty-two, clean-shaven, with thick, very dark hair. He looks so infinitely sad that even Ada is shaken.

Can it be funny?

"Buster Keaton looks sad like that sometimes — don't 'e?"

Ada is reassured.

Buster Keaton looks sad; Buster Keaton is funny. Adam looks sad; Adam is funny. What could be clearer?

The cab stops and Adam gives it all his money. It wishes him "Good night" and disappears into the darkness. Adam unlocks the front door.

On his way upstairs he takes his letters from the hall table; they are two bills and an invitation to a dance.

He reaches his room, undresses and sits for some time wretchedly staring at himself in the glass. Then he gets into bed. He dare not turn out the light because he knows that if he does the room will start spinning round him; he must be there thinking of Imogen until he becomes sober.

The film becomes darker. The room begins to swim and then steadies itself. It is getting quite dark. The orchestra plays softly the first bars of "Everybody loves my baby." It is quite dark.

Close up: the heroine.

Close up: the hero asleep.

Fade out.

NEXT MORNING 8.30 A.M.

The hero still asleep. The electric light is still burning.

A disagreeable-looking maid enters, turns out the light and raises the blind.

Adam wakes up.

"Good morning, Parsons."

"Good morning, sir."

"Is the bathroom empty?"

"I think Miss Jane's just this minute gone along there."

She picks up Adam's evening clothes from the floor.

Adam lies back and ponders the question of whether he shall miss his bath or miss getting a place at the studio.

Miss Jane in her bath.

Adam deciding to get up.

Tired out but with no inclination to sleep, Adam dresses. He goes down to breakfast.

"It can't be Society, Gladys, they aren't eating grapefruit."

"It's such a small 'ouse too."

"And no butler."

"Look, there's 'is little old mother. She'll lead 'im straight in the end. See if she don't."

"Well, that dress isn't at all what I call fashionable, if you ask me."

"Well, if it isn't funny and it isn't murder and it isn't Society, what is it?"

"P'r'aps there'll be a murder yet."

"Well, I calls it soft, that's what I calls it."

"Look now, 'e's got a invitation to a dance from a Countess."

"I don't understand this picture."

The Countess's invitation.

"Why, there isn't even a coronet on it, Ada."

The little old mother pours out tea for him and tells him about the death of a friend in the *Times* that morning; when he has drunk some tea and eaten some fish, she bustles him out of the house.

Adam walks to the corner of the road, where he gets on a bus. The neighbourhood is revealed as being Regent's Park.

THE CENTRE OF LONDON'S QUARTIER LATIN
THE MALTBY SCHOOL OF ART

No trouble has been spared by the producers to obtain the right atmosphere. The top studio at Maltby's is already half full of young students when Adam enters. Work has not yet started, but the room is alive with busy preparation. A young woman in an overall— looking rather more like a chorus girl than a painter—is making herself very dirty cleaning her palette; another near by is setting up an easel; a third is sharpening a pencil; a fourth is smoking a cigarette in a long holder. A young man, also in an overall, is holding a drawing and appraising it at arm's length, his head slightly on one side; a young man with untidy hair is disagreeing with him. Old Mr. Maltby, an inspiring figure in a shabby silk dressing-gown, is telling a tearful student that if she misses another composition class, she will be asked to leave the school. Miss Philbrick, the secretary interrupts the argument between the two young men to remind them that neither of them has paid his fee for the month. The girl who was setting up the easel is trying to borrow some "fixative"; the girl with the cigarette-holder lends her some. Mr. Maltby is complaining of the grittiness of the charcoal they make nowadays. Surely this is the Quartier Latin itself?

The "set," too, has been conscientiously planned. The walls are hung with pots, pans and paintings—these last mainly a series of rather fleshly nudes which young Mr. Maltby has been unable to sell. A very brown skeleton hangs over the dais at the far end.

"I say, Gladys, do you think we shall see 'is models?"

"Coo, Ada, you are a one."

Adam comes in and goes towards the board on which hangs a plan of the easel places; the girl who was lending the "fixative" comes over to him, still smoking.

"THERE'S A PLACE EMPTY NEXT TO ME, DOURE, DO COME THERE."

Close up of the girl.

"She's in love with 'im."

Close up of Adam.

"'E's not in love with 'er, though, is 'e, Ada?"

The place the girl points out is an excellent one in the second row; the only other one besides the very front and very back is round at the side, next to the stove. Adam signs his initials opposite this place.

"I'M SORRY—I'M AFRAID THAT I FIND THE LIGHT WORRIES ME FROM WHERE YOU ARE—ONE GETS SO FEW SHADOWS—DON'T YOU FIND?"

The girl is not to be discouraged; she lights another cigarette.

"I SAW YOU LAST NIGHT AT THE COCKATRICE—YOU DIDN'T SEE ME THOUGH."

"THE COCKATRICE—LAST NIGHT—OH, YES—WHAT A PITY!"

"WHO WERE ALL THOSE PEOPLE YOU WITH WITH?"

"OH, I DON'T KNOW, JUST SOME PEOPLE, YOU KNOW."

He makes a movement as if to go away.

"WHO WAS THAT GIRL YOU WERE DANCING WITH SO MUCH—THE PRETTY ONE WITH FAIR HAIR—IN BLACK?"

"OH, DON'T YOU KNOW HER? YOU MUST MEET HER ONE DAY—I SAY, I'M AWFULLY SORRY, BUT I MUST GO DOWN AND GET SOME PAPER FROM MISS PHILBRICK."

"I CAN LEND YOU SOME."

But he is gone.

Ada says, "Too much talk in this picture, eh, Gladys?" and the voice with the Cambridge accent is heard saying something about the "elimination of the caption."

ONE OF LIFE'S UNFORTUNATES

Enter a young woman huddled in a dressing-gown, preceded by young Mr. Maltby.

"The model—coo—I say."

She has a slight cold and sniffles into a tiny ball of handkerchief; she mounts the dais and sits down ungracefully. Young Mr. Maltby nods good morning to those of the pupils who catch his eye; the girl who was talking to Adam catches his eye; he smiles.

"'E's in love with 'er."

She returns his smile with warmth.

Young Mr. Maltby rattles the stove, opens the skylight a little and then turns to the model, who slips off her dressing-gown and puts it over the back of the chair.

"Coo—I say. Ada—my!"

"Well I never."

The young man from Cambridge goes on talking about Matisse unfalteringly as though he were well accustomed to this sort of thing. Actually he is much intrigued.

She has disclosed a dull pink body with rather short legs and red elbows; like most professional models her toes are covered with bunions and malformed. Young Mr. Maltby sets her on the chair in an established Art School pose. The class settles to work.

Adam returns with some sheets of paper and proceeds to arrange them on his board. Then he stands for some time glaring at the model without drawing a line.

"'E's in love with 'er." But for once Ada's explanation is wrong— and then begins sketching in the main lines of the pose.

He works on for five or six minutes, during which time the heat of the stove becomes increasingly uncomfortable. Old Mr. Maltby, breathing smoke, comes up behind him.

"How have you placed it? What is your centre? Where is the foot going to come? Where is the top of the head coming?"

Adam has not placed it; he rubs it out angrily and starts again.

Meanwhile a vivid flirtation is in progress between young Mr. Maltby and the girl who was in love with Adam. He is leaning over and pointing out mistakes to her; his hand rests on her shoulder; she is wearing a low-necked jumper; his thumb strays over the skin of her neck; she wriggles appreciatively. He takes the charcoal from her and begins drawing in the corner of her paper; her hair touches his cheek; neither of them heed the least what he is drawing.

"These Bo'emians don't 'alf carry on, eh, Gladys?"

In half an hour Adam has rubbed out his drawing three times. Whenever he is beginning to interest himself in some particular combination of shapes, the model raises her ball of handkerchief to her nose, and after each sniff relapses into a slightly different position. The anthracite stove glows with heat; he works on for another half-hour.

THE ELEVEN O'CLOCK REST

Most of the girls light cigarettes; the men, who have increased in number with many late arrivals, begin to congregate away from them in the corner. One of them is reading *The Studio*. Adam lights a pipe, and standing back, surveys his drawing with detestation.

Close up; Adam's drawing. It is not really at all bad. In fact it is by far the best in the room; there is one which will be better at the end of the week, but at present there is nothing of it except some measurements and geometrical figures. Its author is unaware that the model is resting; he is engaged in calculating the medial section of her height in the corner of the paper.

Adam goes out on to the stairs, which are lined with women from the lower studio eating buns out of bags. He returns to the studio.

The girl who has been instructed by young Mr. Maltby comes up to him and looks at his drawing.

"Rather Monday morningish."

That was exactly what young Mr. Maltby had said about hers.

The model resumes her pose with slight differences; the paper bags are put away, pipes are knocked out; the promising pupil is calculating the area of a rectangle.

The scene changes to

158 PONT STREET. THE LONDON HOUSE OF
MR. CHARLES AND LADY ROSEMARY QUEST

An interior is revealed in which the producers have at last made some attempt to satisfy the social expectations of Gladys and Ada. It is true that there is very little marble and no footmen in powder and breeches, but there is nevertheless an undoubted air of grandeur about the high rooms and Louis Seize furniture, and there *is* a footman. The young man from Cambridge estimates the household at six thousand a year, and though somewhat overgenerous, it is a reasonable guess. Lady Rosemary's collection of Limoges can be seen in the background.

Upstairs in her bedroom Imogen Quest is telephoning.

"What a lovely Kimony, Ada."

Miss Philbrick comes into the upper studio at Maltby's, where Adam is at last beginning to take some interest in his drawing.

"MISS QUEST WANTS TO SPEAK TO YOU ON THE TELEPHONE, MR. DOURE. I told her that it was against the rules for students to use the telephone except in the luncheon hour" (there is always a pathetic game of make-believe at Maltby's played endlessly by Miss Philbrick and old Mr. Maltby, in which they pretend that somewhere there is a code of rules which all must observe), "but she says that it is most important. I do wish you would ask your friends not to ring you up in the mornings."

Adam puts down his charcoal and follows her to the office.

There over the telephone is poor Miss Philbrick's notice written in the script writing she learned at night classes in Southhampton Row.

"Students are forbidden to use the telephone during working hours."

"Good morning, Imogen."

"Yes, quite safely—very tired though."

"I can't, Imogen—for one thing I haven't the money."

"No, you can't afford it either. Anyway, I'm dining with Lady R. to-night. You can tell me then, surely?"

"Why not?"

"Who lives there?"

"Not that awful Basil Hay?"

"Well, perhaps he is."

"I used to meet him at Oxford sometimes."

"WELL, IF YOU'RE SURE YOU CAN PAY I'LL COME TO LUNCHEON WITH YOU."

"WHY THERE? IT'S FRIGHTFULLY EXPENSIVE."

"STEAK-TARTARE—WHAT'S THAT?"

The Cambridge voice explains, "Quite raw, you know, with olives and capers and vinegar and things."

"My dear, you'll turn into a werwolf."

"I should love it if you did."

"Yes, I'm afraid I *am* getting a little morbid."

"One-ish. Please don't be too late — I've only three-quarters of an hour."

"Good-bye, Imogen."

So much of the forbidden conversation is audible to Miss Philbrick.

Adam returns to the studio and draws a few heavy and insensitive lines.

He rubs at them but they still show up grubbily in the pores of the paper. He tears up his drawing; old Mr. Maltby remonstrates; young Mr. Maltby is explaining the construction of the foot and does not look up.

Adam attempts another drawing.

Close up of Adam's drawing.

"'E's thinking of 'er." Unerring Ada!

"These films would be so much more convincing if they would only employ decent draughtsmen to do the hero's drawings for him — don't you think?" Bravo, the cultured bourgeoisie!

TWELVE O'CLOCK

There is a repetition of all the excursions of eleven o'clock.

The promising pupil is working out the ratio of two cubes. The girl who has been learning the construction of the foot comes over to him and looks over his shoulder; he starts violently and loses count.

Adam takes his hat and stick and goes out.

Adam on a 'bus.

Adam studying Poussin at the National Gallery.

Close up of Adam studying Poussin.

"'E's thinking of 'er."

The clock at St. Martin-in-the-Fields strikes one. Adam leaves the National Gallery.

TEN MINUTES PAST ONE. THE DINING-ROOM OF THE RESTAURANT DE LA TOUR DE FORCE

Enter Adam; he looks round but as he had expected, Imogen has not yet arrived. He sits down at a table laid for two and waits.

Though not actually in Soho, the Tour de Force gives unmistakably an impression half cosmopolitan, half theatrical, which Ada would sum up in the word "Bo'emian." The tables are well spaced and the wines are excellent though extremely costly.

Adam orders some sherry and waits, dividing his attention be-

tween the door through which Imogen will enter and the con-
templation of a middle-aged political lawyer of repute who at the
next table is trying to keep amused a bored and exquisitely beautiful
youth of eighteen.

QUARTER TO TWO

Enter Imogen.

The people at the other tables say, "Look, there's Imogen Quest. I
can't see what people find in her, can you?" or else, "I wonder who
that is. Isn't she attractive?"

"My dear, I'm terribly late. I am sorry. I've had the *most* awful
morning shopping with Lady R."

She sits down at the table.

"You haven't got to rush back to your school, have you? Because
I'm never going to see you again. The most awful thing has happened—you order lunch, Adam. I'm very hungry. I want to eat a
steak-tartare and I don't want to drink anything."

Adam orders lunch.

"LADY R. SAYS I'M SEEING TOO MUCH OF YOU. ISN'T IT
TOO AWFUL?"

*Gladys at last is quite at home. The film has been classified.
Young love is being thwarted by purse-proud parents.*

Imogen waves aside a wagon of *hors d'oeuvre*.

"We had quite a scene. She came into my room before I was up
and wanted to know all about last night. Apparently she heard me
come in. And, oh Adam, I can't tell you what dreadful things she's
been saying about you. My dear, *what* an odd luncheon—you've
ordered everything I most detest."

Adam drinks soup.

"THAT'S WHY I'M BEING SENT OFF TO THATCH THIS
AFTERNOON. And Lady R. is going to talk to you seriously to-
night. She's put Mary and Andrew off so that she can *get you alone.*
Adam, how can you expect me to eat all this? and you haven't
ordered yourself anything to drink."

Adam eats an omelette alone. Imogen crumbles bread and
talks to him.

"But, my dear, you mustn't say anything against Basil because I
simply adore him, and he's got the loveliest, vulgarest mother—
you'd simply love her."

The steak-tartare is wheeled up and made before them.

Close up; a dish of pulverized and bleeding meat: hands pouring
in immoderate condiments.

"Do you know, Adam, I don't think I do want this after all. It reminds me so of Henry."

HALF-PAST TWO

Adam has finished luncheon.

"SO YOU SEE, DEAR, WE SHALL NEVER, NEVER MEET AGAIN—PROPERLY I MEAN. Isn't it just too like Lady R. for words?"

Imogen stretches out her hand across the table and touches Adam's.

Close up; Adam's hand, a signet ring on the little finger and a smudge of paint on the inside of the thumb. Imogen's hand—very white and manicured—moves across the screen and touches it.

Gladys gives a slight sob.

"YOU DON'T MIND TOO DREADFULLY—DO YOU, ADAM?"

Adam does mind—very much indeed. He has eaten enough to be thoroughly sentimental.

The Restaurant de la Tour de Force is nearly empty. The political barrister has gone his unregenerate way; the waiters stand about restlessly.

Imogen pays the bill and they rise to go.

"Adam, you must come to Euston and see me off. We can't part just like this—for always, can we? Hodges is meeting me there with the luggage."

They get into a taxi.

Imogen puts her hand in his and they sit like this for a few minutes without speaking.

Then Adam leans towards her and they kiss.

Close up: Adam and Imogen kissing. There is a tear (which finds a ready response in Ada and Gladys, who sob uncontrollably) in Adam's eye; Imogen's lips luxuriously disposed by the pressure.

"Like the Bronzino Venus."

"IMOGEN, YOU NEVER REALLY CARED, DID YOU? IF YOU HAD YOU WOULDN'T GO AWAY LIKE THIS. IMOGEN, DID YOU EVER CARE—REALLY?"

"HAVEN'T I GIVEN PROOF THAT I DID. Adam dear, why will you always ask such tiresome questions. Don't you see how impossible it all is? We've only about five minutes before we reach Euston."

They kiss again.

Adam says, "Damn Lady R."

They reach Euston.

Hodges is waiting for them. She has seen about the luggage; she has seen about tickets; she has even bought magazines; there is nothing to be done.

Adam stands beside Imogen waiting for the train to start; she looks at a weekly paper.

"Do look at this picture of Sybil. Isn't it odd? I wonder when she had it taken."

The train is about to start. She gets into the carriage and holds out her hand.

"Good-bye, darling. You will come to mother's dance in June, won't you? I shall be miserable if you don't. Perhaps we shall meet before then. Good-bye."

The train moves out of the station.

Close up. Imogen in the carriage studying the odd photograph of Sybil.

Adam on the platform watching the train disappear.

Fade out.

"Well, Ada, what d'you think of it?"

"Fine."

"It is curious the way that they can never make their heroes and heroines talk like ladies and gentlemen — particularly in moments of emotion."

A QUARTER OF AN HOUR LATER

Adam is still at Euston, gazing aimlessly at a bookstall. The various prospects before him appear on the screen.

Maltby's. The anthracite stove, the model, the amorous student — (*"the Vamp"*), the mathematical student, his own drawing.

Dinner at home. His father, his mother, Parsons, his sister with her stupid, pimply face and her dull jealousy of all Imogen said and did and wore.

Dinner at Pont Street, head to head with Lady Rosemary.

Dinner by himself at some very cheap restaurant in Soho. And always at the end of it, Solitude and the thought of Imogen.

Close up: Adam registering despair gradually turning to resolution.

Adam on a 'bus going to Hanover Gate.

He walks to his home.

Parsons. Parsons opens the door. Mrs. Doure is out; Miss Jane is out; no, Adam does not want any tea.

Adam's room. It is a rather charming one, high at the top of the house, looking over the trees. At full moon the animals in the

Zoological Gardens can be heard from there. Adam comes in and locks the door.

Gladys is there already.

"Suicide, Ada."

"Yes, but she'll come in time to stop 'im. See if she don't."

"Don't you be too sure. This is a queer picture, this is."

He goes to his desk and takes a small blue bottle from one of the pigeon holes.

"What did I tell yer? Poison."

"The ease with which persons in films contrive to provide themselves with the instruments of death . . ."

He puts it down, and taking out a sheet of paper writes.

"Last message to 'er. Gives 'er time to come and save 'im. You see."

"AVE IMPERATRIX IMMORTALIS,
MORITURUS TE SALUTO"

Exquisitely written.

He folds it, puts it in an envelope and addresses it.

Then he pauses, uncertain.

A vision appears:

The door of Adam's room. Mrs. Doure, changed for dinner, comes up to it and knocks; she knocks repeatedly, and in dismay calls for her husband. Professor Doure tries the door and shakes it. Parsons arrives and Jane. After some time the door is forced open; all the time Professor Doure is struggling with it, Mrs. Doure's agitation increases. Jane makes futile attempts to calm her. At last they all burst into the room. Adam is revealed lying dead on the floor. Scene of unspeakable vulgarity involving tears, hysteria, the telephone, the police. Fade out.

Close up. Adam registering disgust.

Another vision:

A native village in Africa on the edge of the jungle; from one of the low thatch huts creeps a man naked and sick to death, his wives lamenting behind him. He draws himself into the jungle to die alone.

"Lor, Gladys. Instruction."

Another vision:

Rome in the time of Petronius. A young patrician reclines in the centre of his guests. The producers have spared no effort in creating an atmosphere of superb luxury. The hall, as if in some fevered imagining of Alma Tadema, is built of marble, richly illumined by

burning Christians. From right and left barbarian slave boys bring
in a course of roasted peacocks. In the centre of the room a slave girl
dances to a puma. Exit several of the guests to the vomitorium.
Unborn pigs stewed in honey and stuffed with truffles and night-
ingales' tongues succeed the peacocks. The puma, inflamed to
sudden passion, springs at the girl and bears her to the ground; he
stands over her, one paw planted upon her breast from which ooze
tiny drops of blood. She lies there on the Alma Tadema marble, her
eyes fixed upon the host in terrified appeal. But he is toying with
one of the serving boys and does not notice her. More guests depart
to the vomitorium. The puma devours the girl. At length, when the
feast is at its height, a basin of green marble is borne in. Water,
steaming and scented, is poured into it. The host immerses his
hand, and a negro woman who, throughout the banquet has
crouched like some angel of death beside his couch, draws a knife
from her loin cloth and buries it deep in his wrist. The water
becomes red in the green marble. The guests rise to go and with
grave courtesy, though without lifting himself from the couch, he
bids them each farewell. Soon he is left alone. The slave boys huddle
together in the corners, their bare shoulders pressed against each
other. Moved by savage desire, the negress begins suddenly to kiss
and gnaw the deadening arm. He motions her listlessly aside. The
martyrs burn lower until there is only a faint glimmer of light in the
great hall. The smell of cooking drifts out into the terrace and is lost
on the night air. The puma can just be discerned licking its paws in
the gloom.

Adam lights a pipe and taps restlessly with the corner of the
envelope on the writing-table. Then he puts the bottle in his pocket
and unlocks the door.

He turns and walks over to his book-shelves and looks through
them. Adam's book-shelves; it is rather a remarkable library for a
man of his age and means. Most of the books have a certain rarity
and many are elaborately bound; there are also old books of considerable value given him from time to time by his father.

He makes a heap on the floor of the best of them.

MR. MACASSOR'S BOOKSHOP

There is about Mr. Macassor's bookshop the appearance of the
private library of an ancient and unmethodical scholar. Books are
everywhere, on walls, floor and furniture, as though laid down at
some interruption and straightway forgotten. First editions and
early illustrated books lie hidden among Sermons and Blue Books

for the earnest adventurer to find. Mr. Macassor hides his treasures with care.

An elderly man is at the moment engaged in investigating a heap of dusty volumes while Mr. Macassor bends longingly over the table engrossed in a treatise on Alchemy. Suddenly the adventurer's back straightens; his search has been rewarded and he emerges into the light, bearing a tattered but unquestionably genuine copy of the first edition of "Hydrotaphia." He asks Mr. Macassor the price. Mr. Macassor adjusts his spectacles and brushes some snuff from his waistcoat and, bearing the book to the door, examines it as if for the first time.

"Ah, yes, a delightful work. Yes, yes, marvellous style," and he turns the pages fondly. "The large stations of the dead," what a noble phrase. He looks at the cover and wipes it with his sleeve. "Why, I had forgotten I had this copy. It used to belong to Horace Walpole, only someone has stolen the bookplate – the rascal. Still, it was only the Orford one – the armorial one, you know. Well, well, sir, since you have found it I suppose you have the right to claim it. Five guineas, shall I say. But I hate to part with it."

The purchaser is a discerning man. Had he seen this same book badly described in a catalogue he would not have paid half this price for it in its present condition, but the excitement of pursuit and the pride of discovery more even than the legends of Strawberry Hill have distorted his sense of values. One cannot haggle with Mr. Macassor as with some mere tradesman in Charing Cross Road. The purchaser pays and goes away triumphant. It is thus that Mr. Macassor's son at Magdalen is able to keep his rooms full of flowers and, during the season, to hunt two days a week.

Enter Adam from a taxi laden with books. Mr. Macassor offers him snuff from an old tortoiseshell box.

"IT'S A SAD THING TO HAVE TO SELL BOOKS, MR. DOURE. Very sad. I remember as if it was yesterday, Mr. Stevenson coming in to me to sell his books, and will you believe it, Mr. Doure, when it came to the point, after we had arranged everything, his heart failed him and he took them all away again. A great book-lover, Mr. Stevenson."

Mr. Macassor adjusts his spectacles and examines, caressingly, but like some morbid lover fastening ghoulishly upon every imperfection.

"Well, and how much were you expecting for these?"

Adam hazards, "Seventeen pounds," but Mr. Macassor shakes his head sadly.

Five minutes later he leaves the shop with ten pounds and gets into his taxi.

PADDINGTON STATION

Adam in the train to Oxford; smoking, his hands deep in his overcoat pockets.

"'E's thinking of 'er."

OXFORD

KNOW YOU HER SECRET NONE CAN UTTER; HERS OF THE BOOK, THE TRIPLE CROWN? Art title showing Book and Triple Crown; also Ox in ford.

General prospect of Oxford from the train showing reservoir, gas works and part of the prison. It is raining.

The station; two Indian students have lost their luggage. Resisting the romantic appeal of several hansom cab-drivers — even of one in a grey billycock hat, Adam gets into a Ford taxi. Queen Street, Carfax, the High Street, Radcliffe Camera in the distance.

"Look, Ada, St. Paul's Cathedral."

King Edward Street. The cab stops and Adam gets out.

LORD BASINGSTOKE'S ROOMS.
KING EDWARD STREET

Interior of Lord Basingstoke's rooms. On the chimney-piece are photographs of Lord Basingstoke's mother and two of Lord Basingstoke's friends, wearing that peculiarly inane and serene smile only found during the last year at Eton and then only in photographs. Some massive glass paper weights and cards of invitation.

On the walls are large coloured caricatures of Basil Hay drawn by himself at Eton, an early nineteenth-century engraving of Lord Basingstoke's home; two unfinished drawings by Ernest Vaughan of the Rape of the Sabines and a wool picture of two dogs and a cat.

Lord Basingstoke, contrary to all expectations, is neither drinking, gaming, nor struggling with his riding boots; he is engaged on writing a Collections Paper for his tutor.

Lord Basingstoke's paper in a pleasant, childish handwriting.

"BRADLAUGH *v.* GOSSETT. THIS FAMOUS TEST CASE FINALLY ESTABLISHED THE DECISION THAT MARSHAL LAW IS UNKNOWN IN ENGLAND."

He crosses out "marshal" and puts "martial"; then sits biting his pen sadly.

"Adam, how lovely; I had no idea you were in Oxford."
They talk for a little while.
"RICHARD, CAN YOU DINE WITH ME TONIGHT. YOU MUST. I'M HAVING A FAREWELL BLIND." Richard looks sadly at his Collections Paper and shakes his head.
"My dear, I simply can't. I've got to get this finished by to-night. I'm probably going to be sent down as it is."
Adam returns to his taxi.

MR. SAYLE'S ROOMS IN MERTON

Flowers, Medici prints and Nonesuch Press editions. Mr. Sayle is playing "L'Après midi d'un Faun" on the gramophone to an American aunt. He cannot dine with Adam.

MR. HENRY QUEST'S ROOMS IN THE UGLIER
PART OF MAGDALEN

The furniture provided by the College has been little changed except for the addition of some rather repulsive cushions. There are photographs of Imogen, Lady Rosemary and Mr. Macassor's son winning the Magdalen Grind. Mr. Henry Quest has just given tea to two freshmen; he is secretary of the J.C.R. His face, through the disability of the camera, looks nearly black, actually it forms a patriotic combination with his Bullingdon tie; he has a fair moustache.

Adam enters and invites him to dinner. Henry Quest does not approve of his sister's friends; Adam cannot stand Imogen's brother; they are always scrupulously polite to each other.
"I'M SORRY, ADAM, THERE'S A MEETING OF THE CHATHAM HERE TO-NIGHT. I SHOULD HAVE LOVED TO, OTHERWISE. Stay and have a cigarette, won't you? Do you know Mr. Trehearne and Mr. Bickerton-Gibbs?"
Adam cannot stop, he has a taxi waiting.
Henry Quest excuses his intrusion to Messrs. Trehearne and Bickerton-Gibbs.

MR. EGERTON-VERSCHOYLE'S ROOMS IN PECKWATER

Mr. Egerton-Verschoyle has been entertaining to luncheon. Adam stirs him with his foot; he turns over and says:
"There's another in the cupboard — corkscrew's behind the thing, you know. . ." and trails off into incoherence.

MR. FURNESS'S ROOMS IN THE NEXT STAIRCASE

They are empty and dark. Mr. Furness has been sent down.

MR. SWITHIN LANG'S ROOMS IN BEAUMONT STREET

Furnished in white and green. Water colours by Mr. Lang of
Whembley, Mentone and Thatch. Some valuable china and a large
number of magazines. A coloured and ornamental decanter of
Cointreau on the chimney-piece and some gold-beaded glasses. The
remains of a tea-party are scattered about the room, and the air is
heavy with cigarette smoke.

Swithin, all in grey, is reading the *Tatler*.

Enter Adam; effusive greetings.

"Adam, do look at this photograph of Sybil Anderson. Isn't it too
funny?"

Adam has seen it.

They sit and talk for some time.

"Swithin, you must come and dine with me to-night—please."

"Adam, I can't. Gabriel's giving a party in Balliol. Won't you be
there? Oh no, of course, you don't know him, do you? He came up
last term—such a dear, and *so* rich. I'm giving some people dinner
first at the Crown. I'd ask you to join us, only I don't honestly think
you'd like them. It is a pity. What about to-morrow? Come over to
dinner at Thame to-morrow."

Adam shakes his head. "I'm afraid I shan't be here," and
goes out.

AN HOUR LATER

Still alone, Adam is walking down the High Street. It has stopped
raining and the lights shine on the wet road. His hand in his pocket
fingers the bottle of poison.

There appears again the vision of the African village and the
lamenting wives.

ST. MARY'S CLOCK STRIKES SEVEN.

Suddenly Adam's step quickens as he is struck by an idea.

MR. ERNEST VAUGHAN'S ROOMS

They stand in the front quadrangle of one of the uglier and less
renowned colleges midway between the lavatories and the chapel.
The window blind has become stuck half-way up the window so that
by day they are shrouded in a twilight as though of the Nether
world, and by night Ernest's light blazes across the quad, revealing

interiors of unsurpassed debauchery. Swithin once said that, like Ernest, Ernest's rooms were a pillar of cloud by day and a pillar of fire by night. The walls are devoid of pictures except for a half-finished drawing of Sir Beelzebub calling for his rum, which, pinned there a term ago, has begun to droop at the corners, and, spattered with drink and leant against by innumerable shoulders, has begun to take on much the same *pattina* as the walls. Inscriptions and drawings, ranging from almost inspired caricature to meaningless or obscene scrawlings, attest Ernest's various stages of drunkenness.

"Who is this Bach? I have not so much as heard of the man. E. V." Runs across the bedroom door in an unsteady band of red chalk, "UT EXULTAT IN COITU ELEPHAS, SIC RICARDUS," surmounting an able drawing of the benign Basingstoke.

A large composition of the Birth of Queen Victoria can be traced over the fireplace. There are broken bottles and dirty glasses and uncorrected galley proofs on the table; on the corner of the chimney piece a beautiful decanter, the broken stopper of which has been replaced by a cork. Ernest is sitting in the broken wicker chair mending the feathers of some darts with unexpected dexterity. He is a short, sturdy young man, with fierce little eyes and a well-formed forehead. His tweeds, stained with drink and paint, have once been well-made, and still preserve a certain distinction. Women undergraduates, on the rare occasions of his appearance at lectures, not infrequently fall in love with him.

"Bolshevist." It is a reasonable mistake, but a mistake. Until his expulsion for overdue subscriptions, Ernest was a prominent member of the Canning.

Adam goes through the gateway into Ernest's College where two or three youths are standing about staring vacantly at the notice-boards. As Adam goes by, they turn around and scowl at him.

"Another of Vaughan's friends."

Their eyes followed him across the quad, to Ernest's rooms.

Ernest is somewhat surprised at Adam's visit, who, indeed, has never shown any very warm affection for him. However, he pours out whisky.

HALF AN HOUR LATER

It has begun to rain again. Dinner is about to be served in Ernest's College and the porch is crowded by a shabby array of gowned young men vacantly staring at the notice-boards. Here and there a glaring suit of "plus fours" proclaims the generosity of the Rhodes Trust. Adam and Ernest make their way through the cluster of men who mutter their disapproval like peasants at the passage of some black magician.

"IT'S NO GOOD TAKING ME TO ANY CLUB, DOURE, I'VE BEEN BLACK-BALLED FOR THE LOT."

"I should imagine that would have happened — even in Oxford."

AN HOUR LATER. AT THE CROWN

Adam and Ernest are just finishing dinner; both show marked signs of intoxication.

The dining-room at the Crown bears little resemblance to Adam's epicurean dream. The walls, pathetically frescoed with views of Oxford, resound with the clattering of dirty plates. Swithin's dinner-party has just left, leaving the room immeasurably more quiet. The three women who up till now have been playing selections from Gilbert and Sullivan in the corner have finished work and begun eating their dinner. An undergraduate who has very grandly signed the bill is engaged in an argument with the manager. At a table near Adam's three young men with gowns wound round their throats have settled themselves and ordered coffee and cream cakes; while they are waiting they discuss the union elections.

Adam orders more double whiskies.

Ernest insists on sending a bottle of gin over to the party at the next table. It is rejected with some resentment, and soon they rise and go away.

Adam orders more double whiskies.

Ernest begins drawing a portrait of Adam on the table-cloth.

He entitles it *"Le vin triste,"* and, indeed, throughout dinner, Adam has been growing sadder and sadder as his guest has grown more happy. He drinks and orders more with a mechanical weariness.

At length, very unsteady, they rise to go.

From now onwards the film becomes a series of fragmentary scenes interspersed among hundreds of feet of confusion.

"It's going queer again, Ada. D'you think it's meant to be like this?"

A public-house in the slums. Adam leans against the settee and pays for innumerable pints of beer for armies of ragged men. Ernest is engrossed in a heated altercation about birth control with a beggar whom he has just defeated at "darts."

Another public-house: Ernest, beset by two panders, is loudly maintaining the abnormality of his tastes. Adam finds a bottle of

gin in his pocket and attempts to give it to a man; his wife interposes; eventually the bottle falls to the floor and is broken.

Adam and Ernest in a taxi; they drive from college to college,
being refused admission. Fade out.

GABRIEL'S PARTY in Balliol is being an enormous success. It is a
decorous assembly mostly sober. There are bottles of champagne
and decanters of whisky and brandy, but most of Gabriel's guests
prefer dancing. Others sit about and talk. They are large, well-
furnished rooms, and the effect is picturesque and agreeable. There
are a few people in fancy dress — a Queen Victoria, a Sapphist and
two Generals Gordon. A musical comedy actor, who is staying the
week-end with Gabriel, stands by the gramophone looking through
the records; as becomes a guest of honour he is terribly bored.

Henry Quest has escaped from the Chatham and is talking about
diplomatic appointments, drinking whisky and regarding everyone
with disapproval. Lord Basingstoke stands talking to him, with his
mind still worrying about the Constitution of the Commonwealth
of Australia. Swithin is making himself quite delightful to the guest
of honour. Mr. Egerton-Verschoyle sits very white, complaining of
the cold.

Enter Mr. Sayle of Merton.

"GABRIEL, DO LOOK WHO I'VE FOUND IN THE QUAD.
MAY I BRING HIM IN?" He pulls in Adam, who stands with a
broken gin bottle in one hand staring stupidly about the room.

Someone pours him out a glass of champagne.

The party goes on.

A voice is heard roaring "ADAM" outside the window, and
suddenly there bursts in Ernest, looking incredibly drunk. His hair
is disordered, his eyes glazed, his neck and face crimson and greasy.
He sits down in a chair immobile; someone gives him a drink; he
takes it mechanically and then pours it into the carpet and continues
to stare before him.

"ADAM, IS THIS IMPOSSIBLE PERSON A FRIEND OF
YOURS? DO FOR GOODNESS' SAKE TAKE HIM AWAY.
GABRIEL WILL BE FURIOUS."

"HE'S THE MOST MARVELLOUS MAN, HENRY. YOU JUST
DON'T KNOW HIM. COME AND TALK TO HIM."

And to his intense disgust Henry is led across the room and
introduced to Ernest. Ernest at first does not seem to hear, and then
slowly raises his eyes until they are gazing at Henry; by a further
effort he continues to focus them.

"QUEST? ANY RELATION TO ADAM'S WOMAN?"

There is about to be a scene. The musical comedy actor feels that only this was needed to complete the melancholy of the evening. Henry is all indignation and contempt. "IMOGEN QUEST IS MY SISTER IF THAT'S WHAT YOU MEAN. WHO THE DEVIL ARE YOU AND WHAT DO YOU MEAN BY SPEAKING ABOUT HER LIKE THAT?"

Gabriel flutters ineffectually in the background. Richard Basingstoke interposes with a genial, "Come on, Henry, can't you see the frightful man's blind drunk?" Swithin begs Adam to take Ernest away. Everybody is thrown into the utmost agitation.

But Ernest, in his own way, saves everyone from further anxiety. "DO YOU KNOW, I THINK I'M GOING TO BE SICK?"

And makes his way unmolested and with perfect dignity to the quad. The gramophone starts playing "Everybody loves my baby." Fade out.

THE OXFORD CITY LIBERAL ASSOCIATION
DANCE AT THE TOWN HALL

Tickets are being sold at the door for 1s. 6d.

Upstairs there is a table with jugs of lemonade and plates of plum cake. In the main hall a band is playing and the younger liberals are dancing. One of the waitresses from the Crown sits by the door fanning her face with a handkerchief.

Ernest, with a radiant smile, is slowly walking round the room offering plum cake to the couples sitting about. Some giggle and take it; some giggle and refuse; some refuse and look exceedingly haughty.

Adam leans against the side of the door watching him.

Close up; Adam bears on his face the same expression of blind misery that he wore in the taxi the night before.

LE VIN TRISTE

Ernest has asked the waitress from the Crown to dance with him. It is an ungainly performance; still sublimely contented he collides with several couples, misses his footing and, but for his partner, would have fallen. An M.C. in evening dress asks Adam to take him away.

Broad stone steps.

Several motors are drawn up outside the Town Hall. Ernest climbs into the first of them—a decrepit Ford—and starts the engine. Adam attempts to stop him. A policeman hurries up. There is a wrenching of gears and the car starts.

The policeman blows his whistle.

Half-way down St. Aldgates the car runs into the kerb, mounts the pavement and runs into a shop window. The inhabitants of St. Aldgates converge from all sides; heads appear at every window; policemen assemble. There is a movement in the crowd to make way for something being carried out.

Adam turns and wanders aimlessly towards Carfax.

St. Mary's clock strikes twelve.

It is raining again.

Adam is alone.

HALF AN HOUR LATER. AN HOTEL BEDROOM

Adam is lying on his face across the bed, fully clothed. He turns over and sits up. Again the vision of the native village; the savage has dragged himself very near to the edge of the jungle. His back glistens in the evening sun with his last exertion. He raises himself to his feet, and with quick unsteady steps reaches the first bushes; soon he is lost to view.

Adam steadies himself at the foot of the bed and walks to the dressing-table; he leans for a long time looking at himself in the glass.

He walks to the window and looks out into the rain.

Finally he takes the blue bottle from his pocket, uncorks it, smells it, and then without more ado drinks its contents. He makes a wry face at its bitterness and stands for a minute uncertain. Then moved by some odd instinct he turns out the light and curls himself up under the coverlet.

At the foot of a low banyan tree the savage lies very still. A large fly settles on his shoulder; two birds of prey perch on the branch above him, waiting. The tropical sun begins to set, and in the brief twilight animals begin to prowl upon their obscene questings. Soon it is dark.

A photograph of H.M. the King in naval uniform flashes out into the night.

GOD SAVE THE KING

The cinema quickly empties.

The young man from Cambridge goes his way to drink a glass of Pilsen at Odenino's.

Ada and Gladys pass out through ranks of liveried attendants.

For perhaps the fiftieth time in the course of the evening Gladys says, "Well, I do call it a soft film."

"Fancy 'er not coming in again."

There is quite a crowd outside, all waiting to go to Earls Court. Ada and Gladys fight manfully and secure places on the top of the 'bus.

"'Ere, 'oo are yer pushing? Mind out, can't yer?"

When they arrive home they will no doubt have some cocoa before going to bed, and perhaps some bread and bloater paste. It has been rather a disappointing evening on the whole. Still, as Ada says, with the pictures you has to take the bad with the good.

Next week there may be something really funny.

Larry Semon or Buster Keaton — who knows?

Conclusion
I

The tea grew cold upon the chamber cupboard and Adam Doure stared out into the void.

The rain of yesterday had cleared away and the sun streamed into the small bedroom, lighting it up with amiable and unwelcome radiance. The distressing sound of a self-starter grappling in vain with a cold engine rang up from the yard below the window. Otherwise everything was quiet.

He cogitated: therefore he was.

From the dismal array of ills that confronted him and the confused memories that lay behind, this one proposition obtruded itself with devastating insistence. Each of his clearing perceptions advanced fresh evidence of his existence; he stretched out his limbs fully clothed under the counterpane and gazed at the ceiling with uncomprehending despair, while memories of the preceding evening, of Ernest Vaughan with swollen neck and staring eye, of the slum bar and the eager faces of the two pimps, of Henry, crimson and self-righteous, of shop girls in silk blouses eating plum cake, of the Ford wrecked in the broken window, fought for precedence in his awakening consciousness until they were established in some fairly coherent chronological order; but always at the end there remained the blue bottle and the sense of finality rudely frustrated. It stood upon the dressing-table now, emptied of all its power of reprieve, while the tea grew cold upon the chamber cupboard.

After all the chaotic impressions which he has thus painfully and imperfectly set in order, the last minutes before he had turned out the light stood out perfectly clearly. He could see the white, inconsolable face that had stared out at him from the looking-glass; he could feel at the back of his tongue the salt and bitter taste of the poison. And then as the image of the taste began to bulk larger in his field of consciousness, as though with the sudden breaking down of some intervening barrier another memory swept in on him blotting out all else with its intensity. He remembered as in a nightmare, remote, yet infinitely clear, his awakening in the darkness with the coldness of death about his heart; he had raised himself from the bed and stumbled to the window and leant there, he did not know how long, with the cold air in his face and the steady monotone of the rain fighting with the drumming of blood in his head. Gradually, as he stood there motionless, nausea had come upon him; he had fought it back, his whole will struggling in the effort; it had come again; his drunken senses relaxed their resistance, and with complete abandonment of purpose and restraint, he vomited into the yard below.

Slowly and imperceptibly the tea grew cold on the chamber cupboard.

II

Centuries ago, in his dateless childhood, Ozymandias had sprung to the top of the toy cupboard tired of Adam's game. It was a game peculiar to himself and Ozymandias which Adam had evolved, and which was only played on the rare occasions of his being left alone. First, Ozymandias had to be sought from room to room, and when at last he was found, borne up to the nursery and shut in. He would watch him for some minutes as he paced the floor and surveyed the room with just the extreme tip of his tail expressing his unfathomable contempt for European civilization. Then armed with a sword, gun, battledore, or an armful of bricks to throw, and uttering sadistic cries, Adam would pursue him round and round the room, driving him from refuge to refuge, until almost beside himself with rage and terror, he crouched jungle-like with ears flattened back and porpentine hair. Here Adam would rest, and after some slight pause the real business of the game began. Ozymandias had to be won back to complacency and affection. Adam would sit down on the floor some little way from him and begin calling to him softly and endearingly. He would lie on his stomach with his face as near Ozymandias as he would allow and whisper extravagant eulogies of his beauty and grace; mother-like he would comfort him, evoking some fictitious tormentor to be reproached, assuring him that he was powerless to hurt him any more; Adam would protect him; Adam would see that the horrible little boy did not come near him again. Slowly Ozymandias' ears would begin to come forward and his eyes begin to close, and the delectable exercise invariably ended with caresses of passionate reconciliation.

On this particular afternoon, however, Ozymandias had refused to play, and the moment Adam brought him into the nursery had established himself in unassailable sanctuary at the top of the toy cupboard. He sat there among the dust and broken toys, and Adam, foiled in his purpose, sat gloomily beneath calling to him. But Adam — at the age of seven — was not easily discouraged, and soon began pushing up the nursery table towards the cupboard. This done, he lifted the soldier box into it, and above this planted a chair. There was not room, turn it how he might, for all four legs to rest on the box, but content with an unstable equilibrium, Adam poised it upon three and mounted. When his hands were within a few inches of Ozymandias' soft fur an unwary step on to the unsupported part of the chair precipitated him and it, first on to the table and then with a clatter and cry on to the floor.

Adam had been too well brought up to remember very much of his life in the days before he went to his private school, but this incident survived in his memory with a clearness, which increased as he became farther removed from it, as the first occasion on which he became conscious of ill as a subjective entity. His life up till this time had been so much bounded with warnings of danger that it seemed for a moment inconceivable that he could so easily have broken through into the realm of positive bodily harm. Indeed, so incompatible did it seem with all previous experience that it was some appreciable time before he could convince himself of the continuity of his existence; but for the wealth of Hebraic and mediæval imagery with which the idea of life outside the body had become symbolized, he could in that moment easily have believed in his own bodily extinction and the unreality of all the sensible objects about him. Later he learned to regard these periods between his fall and the dismayed advent to help from below, as the first promptings towards that struggle for detachment in which he had not, without almost frantic endeavour, finally acknowledged defeat in the bedroom of the Oxford hotel.

The first phase of detachment had passed and had been succeeded by one of methodical investigation. Almost simultaneously with his acceptance of his continued existence had come the conception of pain — vaguely at first as of a melody played by another to which his senses were only fitfully attentive, but gradually taking shape as the tangible objects about him gained in reality, until at length it appeared as a concrete thing, external but intimately attached to himself. Like the pursuit of quicksilver with a spoon, Adam was able to chase it about the walls of his consciousness until at length he drove it into a corner in which he could examine it at his leisure. Still lying perfectly still, just as he had fallen, with his limbs half embracing the wooden legs of the chair, Adam was able, by concentrating his attention upon each part of his body in turn, to exclude the disordered sensations to which his fall had given rise and trace the several constituents of the bulk of pain down their vibrating channels to their sources in his various physical injuries. The process was nearly complete when the arrival of his nurse dissolved him into tears and scattered his bewildered ratiocinations.

It was in some such mood as this that, an hour or so after his awakening, Adam strode along the towing path away from Oxford. He still wore the clothes in which he had slept, but in his intellectual dishevelment he had little concern for his appearance. All about him the shadows were beginning to dissipate and give place to clearer images. He had breakfasted in a world of phantoms, in a great room full of uncomprehending eyes, protruding grotesquely from monstrous heads that lolled over steaming porridge; marionette waiters had pirouetted about him with uncouth gestures. All round him a macabre dance of shadows had reeled and flickered, and in and out of it Adam had picked his way, conscious only of one insistent need, percolating through to him from the world outside, of immediate escape from the scene upon which the bodiless harlequinade was played, into a third dimension beyond it.

And at length, as he walked by the river, the shapes of the design began to advance and recede, and the pattern about him and the shadows of the night before became planes and masses and arranged themselves into a perspective, and like the child in the nursery Adam began feeling his bruises.

Somewhere among the red roofs across the water bells were ringing discordantly.

Two men were fishing on the bank. They looked curiously at him and returned their attention to their barren sport.

A small child passed him sucking her thumb in Freudian ecstasy.

And after a time Adam left the footpath and lay down under a bank and by the grace of God fell asleep.

III

It was not a long or an unbroken sleep, but Adam rose from it refreshed and after a little while resumed his journey.

On a white footbridge he paused, and lighting his pipe, gazed down into his ruffled image. A great swan swept beneath him with Spenserian grace, and as the scattered particles of his reflection began to reassemble, looking more than ever grotesque in contrast with the impeccable excellence of the bird, he began half-consciously to speak aloud:

"So, you see, you are after all come to the beginning of another day." And as he spoke, he took from his pocket the envelope addressed to Imogen and tore it into small pieces. Like wounded birds they tumbled and fluttered, until reaching the water they became caught up in its movement and were swept out of sight round the bend of the river towards the city, which Adam had just left.

The reflection answered: "Yes, I think that that was well done. After all, 'imperatrix' is not a particularly happy epithet to apply to Imogen, is it? — and, by the way, are you certain that she can understand Latin? Suppose that she had had to ask Henry to translate it to her!

"But, tell me, does this rather picturesque gesture mean that you have decided to go on living? You seemed so immovably resolved on instant death yesterday, that I find it hard to believe you can have changed your mind."

Adam: I find it hard to believe that it was I who yesterday was so immovably resolved. I cannot explain but it seems to me as though the being who survives, I must admit, with very great clearness in my memory, was born of a dream, drank and died in a dream.

The Reflection: And loved in a dream, too?

Adam: There you confound me, for it seems to me that that love of his alone does partake of reality. But perhaps I am merely yielding to the intensity of the memory. Indeed I think that I am. For the rest that being had no more substance than you yourself, whom the passage of a bird can dissolve.

Reflection: That is a sorry conclusion, for I am afraid that you are trying to dismiss as a shadow a being in every way as real as yourself. But in your present mood it would be useless to persuade you. Tell me instead, what was the secret which you learned, asleep there in the grass?

Adam: I found no secret — only a little bodily strength.

Reflection: Is the balance of life and death so easily swayed?

Adam: It is the balance of appetite and reason. The reason remains constant — the appetite varies.

Reflection: And is there no appetite for death?

Adam: None which cannot be appeased by sleep or change or the mere passing of time.

Reflection: And in the other scale no reason?

Adam: None. None.

Reflection: No honour to be observed to friends? No inter-penetration, so that you cannot depart without bearing away with you something that is part of another?

Adam: None.

Reflection: Your art?

Adam: Again the appetite to live — to preserve in the shapes of things the personality whose dissolution you foresee inevitably.

Reflection: That is the balance then — and in the end circumstance decides.

Adam: Yes, in the end circumstance.

Continuation

They have all come over to Thatch for the day; nine of them, three in Henry Quest's Morris and the others in a huge and shabby car belonging to Richard Basingstoke. Mrs. Hay had only expected Henry Quest and Swithin, but she waves a plump hand benignly and the servants busy themselves in finding more food. It is so nice living near Oxford, and Basil's friends always *look* so charming about the place even if they are rather odd in their manners sometimes. They all talk so quickly that she can never hear what they are saying and they never finish their sentences either — but it doesn't matter, because they always talk about people she doesn't know. Dear boys, of course they don't mean to be rude really — they are so well bred, and it *is* nice to see them making themselves really at home. Who are they talking about now?

"No, Imogen, *really*, he's getting rather impossible."

"I can't tell you what he was like the other night."

"The night you came down here."

"Gabriel was giving a party."

"And he didn't know Gabriel and he hadn't been asked."

"And Gabriel didn't want him — did you, Gabriel?"

"Because you never know what he is going to do next."

"And he brought in the *most dreadful* person."

"Quite, quite drunk."

"Called Ernest Vaughan, you wouldn't have met him. Just the *most awful* person in the world. Gabriel was perfectly sweet to him."

Dear boys, so young, so intolerant.

Still, if they must smoke between courses, they might be a little more careful with the ash. The dark boy at the end—Basil always forgot to introduce his friends to her—was quite ruining the table.

"Edwards, give the gentleman next to Lord Basingstoke another ash-tray."

What were they saying?

"D'you know, Henry, I think that that was rather silly of you? Why should I mind what some poor drunk says about me?"

What a sweet girl Imogen Quest was. So much *easier* than her father. Mrs. Hay was always rather afraid of Imogen's father. She was afraid Henry was going to be like him. How charming she looks now. She cannot understand why all the boys aren't in love with her. When Mrs. Hay was young, they would have been. None of Basil's friends seemed quite the "marrying sort" somehow. Now if only Basil would marry someone like Imogen Quest. . . .

"But do you know, I think I've met Ernest Vaughan? Or at least someone pointed him out to me once. Didn't you, Swithin?"

"Yes. You said you thought he was rather attractive."

"Imogen!"

"My dear."

"I think he is. Isn't he short and dirty with masses of hair?"

"Always drunk."

"Yes, I remember. I think he looked very charming. I want to meet him properly."

"Imogen, you can't, *really*. He is *too* awful."

"Didn't he do those pictures in Richard's room? Richard, will you invite me to meet him one day?"

"No, Imogen, really I couldn't."

"Then someone must—Gabriel, you will, *please*. I insist on meeting him."

Dear children, so young, so *chic*.

"Well, I think it's perfectly beastly of you all. But I will meet him all the same. I'll get Adam to arrange it."

The table was ruined.

"Edwards, I think it's almost fine enough to have coffee outside."

37

The Tutor's Tale:
A House of
Gentlefolks

[On February 20, 1927, the day that Waugh was fired from his teaching job at Aston Clinton school, he received an offer of ten guineas for a story. The story was completed and accepted by March 7 (*Diaries*, pp. 280–82.) Text: *The New Decameron: The Fifth Day*, ed. Hugh Chesterman (Oxford: Basil Blackwell, 1927), pp. 101–16. The final section of the story, probably written by Chesterman, links this to the next tale in the volume.]

I arrived at Vanburgh at five to one. It was raining hard by now and the dreary little station yard was empty except for a deserted and draughty-looking taxi. They might have sent a car for me.

How far was it to Stayle? About three miles, the ticket collector told me. Which part of Stayle might I be wanting? The Duke's? That was a good mile the other side of the village.

They really might have sent a car.

With a little difficulty I found the driver of the taxi, a sulky and scorbutic young man who may well have been the bully of some long-forgotten school story. It was some consolation to feel that he must be getting wetter than I. It was a beastly drive.

After the cross-roads at Stayle we reached what were obviously the walls of the park, interminable and dilapidated walls that stretched on past corners and curves with leafless trees dripping on to their dingy masonry. At last they were broken by lodges and gates, four gates and three lodges, and through the ironwork I could see a great sweep of ill-kept drive.

But the gates were shut and padlocked and most of the windows in the lodges were broken.

"There are some more gates further on," said the school bully, "and beyond them, and beyond them again. I suppose they must get in and out somehow, sometimes."

At last we found a white wooden gate and a track which led

through some farm buildings into the main drive. The park land on either side was railed off and no doubt let out to pasture. One very dirty sheep had strayed on to the drive and stumbled off in alarm at our approach, continually looking over its shoulder and then starting away again until we overtook it. Last of all the house came in sight, spreading out prodigiously in all directions.

The man demanded eight shillings for the fare. I gave it to him and rang the bell.

After some delay an old man opened the door to me.

"Mr. Vaughan," I said. "I think his Grace is expecting me to luncheon."

"Yes; will you come in, please?" and I was just handing him my hat when he added: "I am the Duke of Vanburgh. I hope you will forgive my opening the door myself. The butler is in bed to-day— he suffers terribly in his back during the winter, and both my footmen have been killed in the war." *Have been killed*—the words haunted me incessantly throughout the next few hours and for days to come. That desolating perfect tense, after ten years at least, probably more . . . Miss Stein and the continuous present; the Duke of Vanburgh and the continuous perfect passive. . . .

I was unprepared for the room to which he led me. Only once before, at the age of twelve, had I been to a ducal house, and besides the fruit garden, my chief memory of that visit was one of intense cold and of running upstairs through endless passages to get my mother a fur to wear around her shoulders after dinner. It is true that that was in Scotland, but still I was unprepared for the overpowering heat that met us as the Duke opened the door. The double windows were tight shut and a large coal fire burned brightly in the round Victorian grate. The air was heavy with the smell of chrysanthemums, there was a gilt clock under a glass case on the chimney-piece and everywhere in the room stiff little assemblages of china and bric-à-brac. One might expect to find such a room in Lancaster Gate or Elm Park Gardens where the widow of some provincial knight knits away her days among trusted servants. In front of the fire sat an old lady, eating an apple.

"My dear, this is Mr. Vaughan, who is going to take Stayle abroad—my sister, Lady Emily. Mr. Vaughan has just driven down from London in his motor."

"No," I said, "I came by train—the 12.55."

"Wasn't that very expensive?" said Lady Emily.

Perhaps I ought here to explain the reason for my visit. As I have said, I am not at all in the habit of moving in these exalted circles, but I have a rather grand godmother who shows a sporadic interest in my affairs. I had just come down from Oxford, and was very much at a loose end when she learned unexpectedly that the Duke of Vanburgh was in need of a tutor to take his grandson and heir abroad — a youth called the Marquess of Stayle, eighteen years old. It had seemed a tolerable way in which to spend the next six months, and accordingly the thing had been arranged. I was here to fetch away my charge and start for the Continent with him next day.

"Did you say you came by train?" said the Duke.

"By the 12.55."

"But you said you were coming by motor."

"No, really, I can't have said that. For one thing I haven't got a motor."

"But if you hadn't said that, I should have sent Byng to meet you. Byng didn't meet you, did he?"

"No," I said, "he did not."

"Well, there you see."

Lady Emily put down the core of her apple and said very suddenly:

"Your father used to live at Oakshott. I knew him quite well. Shocking bad on a horse."

"No, that was my uncle Hugh. My father was in India almost all his life. He died there."

"Oh, I don't think he can have done that," said Lady Emily; "I don't believe he even went there — did he, Charles?"

"Who? what?"

"Hugh Vaughan never went to India, did he?"

"No, no, of course not. He sold Oakshott and went to live in Hampshire somewhere. He never went to India in his life."

At this moment another old lady, almost indistinguishable from Lady Emily, came into the room.

"This is Mr. Vaughan, my dear. You remember his father at Oakshott, don't you? He's going to take Stayle abroad — my sister, Lady Gertrude."

Lady Gertrude smiled brightly and took my hand.

"Now I knew there was someone coming to luncheon, and then I saw Byng carrying in the vegetables a quarter of an hour ago. I thought, now he ought to be at Vanburgh meeting the train."

"No, no, dear," said Lady Emily. "Mr. Vaughan came down by motor."

"Oh, that's a good thing. I thought he said he was coming by train."

II

The Marquess of Stayle did not come in to luncheon.

"I am afraid you may find him rather shy at first," explained the Duke. "We did not tell him about your coming until this morning. We were afraid it might unsettle him. As it is he is a little upset about it. Have you seen him since breakfast, my dear?"

"Don't you think," said Lady Gertrude, "that Mr. Vaughan had better know the truth about Stayle? He is bound to discover it soon."

The Duke sighed: "The truth is, Mr. Vaughan, that my grandson is not quite right in his head. Not mad, you understand, but noticeably underdeveloped."

I nodded. "I gathered from my godmother that he was a little backward."

"That is largely why he never went to school. He went to a private school once for two terms, but he was very unhappy and the fees were very high; so I took him away. Since then he has had no regular education."

"No education of any sort, dear," said Lady Gertrude gently.

"Well, it practically amounts to that. And it is a sad state of affairs, as you will readily understand. You see, the boy will succeed me and — well, it is very unfortunate. Now there is quite a large sum of money which his mother left for the boy's education. Nothing has been done with it — to tell you the truth, I had forgotten all about it until my lawyer reminded me of it the other day. It is about thirteen hundred pounds by now, I think. I have talked the matter over with Lady Emily and Lady Gertrude, and we came to the conclusion that the best thing to do would be to send him abroad for a year with a tutor. It might make a difference. Anyway, we shall feel that we have done our duty by the boy." (It seemed to me odd that they should feel that about it, but I said nothing.) "You will probably have to get him some clothes too. You see he has never been about much, and we have let him run wild a little, I am afraid."

When luncheon was over they brought out a large box of peppermint creams. Lady Emily ate five.

III

Well, I had been sent down from Oxford with every circumstance of discredit, and it did not become me to be over nice; still, to spend a year conducting a lunatic nobleman about Europe was rather more than I had bargained for. I had practically made up my mind to risk my godmother's displeasure and throw up the post while there was still time, when the young man made his appearance.

He stood at the door of the dining-room surveying the four of us, acutely ill at ease but with a certain insolence.

"Hullo, have you finished lunch? May I have some peppermints, Aunt Emily?"

He was not a bad-looking youth at all, slightly over middle height, and he spoke with that rather agreeable intonation that gentlepeople acquire who live among servants and farm hands. His clothes, with which he had obviously been at some pains, were unbelievable — a shiny blue suit with four buttons, much too small for him, showing several inches of wrinkled woollen sock and white flannel shirt. About this he had put on a stiff evening collar and a very narrow tie, tied in a sailor-knot. His hair was far too long, and he had been putting water on it. But for all this he did not look mad.

"Come and say, 'How do you do?' to your new tutor," said Lady Gertrude, as though to a child of six. "Give him your right hand — that's it."

He came awkwardly toward me, holding out his hand, then put it behind him and then shot it out again suddenly, leaning his body forward as he did so. I felt a sudden shame for this poor ungraceful creature.

"How-d'you-do?" he said. "I expect they forgot to send the car for you, didn't they? The last tutor walked out and didn't get here until half-past two. Then they said I was mad, so he went away again. Have they told you I'm mad yet?"

"No," I said decidedly, "of course not."

"Well, they will then. But perhaps they have already, and you didn't like to tell me. You're a gentleman, aren't you? That's what grandfather said: 'He's a bad hat, but at least he's a gentleman.' But you needn't worry about me. They all say I'm mad."

Anywhere else this might have caused some uneasiness, but the placid voice of Lady Gertrude broke in:

"Now, you mustn't talk like that to Mr. Vaughan. Come and have a peppermint, dear." And she looked at me as though to say, "What did I tell you?"

Quite suddenly I decided to take on the job after all.

An hour later we were in the train. I had the Duke's cheque for £150 preliminary expenses in my pocket; the boy's preposterous little wicker box was in the rack over his head.

"I say," he said, "what am I to call you?"

"Well, most of my friends call me Ernest."

"May I really do that?"

"Yes, of course. What shall I call you?"

He looked doubtful. "Grandfather and the aunts call me Stayle; everyone else calls me 'my Lord' when they are about and 'Bats' when we are alone. It's short for 'Bats in the Belfrey,' you know."

"But haven't you got a Christian name?"

He had to think before he answered. "Yes—George Theodore Verney."

"Well, I'm going to call you George."

"Will you really? I say, have you been to London a lot?"

"Yes, I live there usually."

"I say. D'you know I've never been to London? I've never been away from home at all—except to that school."

"Was that beastly?"

"It was ——" He used a ploughboy's oath. "I say, oughtn't I to say that? Aunt Emily says I shouldn't."

"She's quite right."

"Well, she's got some mighty queer ideas, I can tell you," and for the rest of the journey he chatted freely. That evening he evinced a desire to go to a theatre, but remembering his clothes, I sent him to bed early and went out in search of friends. I felt that with £150 in my pocket I could afford champagne. Besides, I had a good story to tell.

We spent the next day ordering clothes. It was clear the moment I saw his luggage that we should have to stay on in London for four or five days; he had nothing that he could possibly wear. As soon as he was up I put him into one of my overcoats and took him to all the shops where I owed money. He ordered lavishly and with evident relish. By the evening the first parcels had begun to arrive and his room was a heap of cardboard and tissue-paper. Mr. Phillrick, who always gives me the impression that I am the first commoner who has dared to order a suit from him, so far relaxed from his customary austerity as to call upon us at the hotel, followed by an assistant with a large suitcase full of patterns. George showed a well-bred leaning towards checks. Mr. Phillrick could get two suits finished by Thursday. The other would follow us to the Crillon. Did he know anywhere where we could get a tolerable suit of evening clothes ready made? He gave us the name of the shop where his firm sold their misfits. He remembered his Lordship's father well. He would call upon his Lordship for a fitting to-morrow evening. Was I sure that I had all the clothes I needed at the moment? He had some

patterns just in. As for that little matter of my bill — of course, any
time that was convenient to me. (His last letter had made it unmistakably clear that he must have a cheque on account before
undertaking any further orders.) I ordered two suits. All of this
George enjoyed enormously.

After the first morning I gave up all attempt at a tutorial attitude.
We had four days to spend in London before we could start and, as
George had told me, it was his first visit. He had an unbounded zeal
to see everything, and, above all, to meet people; but he had also a
fresh and acute critical faculty and a natural fastidiousness which
shone through the country bumpkin. The first time he went to a
revue he was all agog with excitement; the theatre, the orchestra,
the audience all enthralled him. He insisted on being there ten
minutes before the time; he insisted on leaving ten minutes before
the end of the first act. He thought it vulgar and dull and ugly, and
there was so much else that he was eager to see. The dreary "might-
as-well-stay-here-now-we've-paid" attitude was unintelligible to
him.

In the same way with his food, he wished to try all the dishes. If he
found he did not like anything, he ordered something else. On the
first evening we dined out he decided that champagne was tasteless
and disagreeable and refused to drink it again. He had no patience
for acquiring tastes, but most good things pleased him immediately. At the National Gallery he would look at nothing after
Bellini's "Death of Peter Martyr."

He was an immediate success with everyone I introduced him to.
He had no "manner" of any kind. He said all he thought with very
little reticence and listened with the utmost interest to all he heard
said. At first he would sometimes break in with rather disturbing
sincerity upon the ready-made conversations with which we are
mostly content, but almost at once he learned to discern what was
purely mechanical and to disregard it. He would pick up tags and
phrases and use them with the oddest twists, revitalising them by his
interest in their picturesqueness.

And all this happened in four days; if it had been in four months
the change would have been remarkable. I could see him develop-
ing from one hour to the next.

On our last evening in London I brought out an atlas and tried to
explain where we were going. The world for him was divided
roughly into three hemispheres — Europe, where there had been a
war; it was full of towns like Paris and BudaPest, all equally remote
and peopled with prostitutes; the East, a place full of camels and

elephants, deserts and dervishes and nodding mandarins; and America, which besides its own two continents included Australia, New Zealand, and most of the British Empire not obviously "Eastern"; somewhere, too, there were some "savages."

"We shall have to stop the night at Brindisi," I was saying. "then we can get the Lloyd Trestino in the morning. What a lot you're smoking!"

We had just returned from a tea and cocktail party. George was standing at the looking-glass gazing at himself in his new clothes.

"You know, he has made this suit rather well, Ernest. It's about the only thing I learned at home — smoking, I mean. I used to go up to the saddle-room with Byng."

"You haven't told me what you thought of the party."

"Ernest, why are all your friends being so sweet to me? Is it just because I'm going to be a duke?"

"I expect that makes a difference with some of them — Julia for instance. She said you looked so fugitive."

"I'm afraid I didn't like Julia much. No, I mean Peter and that funny Mr. Oliphant."

"I think they like you."

"How odd!" He looked at himself in the glass again. "D'you know, I'll tell you something I've been thinking all these last few days. I don't believe I really am mad at all. It's only at home I feel so different from everyone else. Of course I don't know much . . . I've been thinking, d'you think it can be grandfather and the aunts who are mad, all the time?"

"They're certainly getting old."

"No, mad. I can remember some awfully dotty things they've done at one time or another. Last summer Aunt Gertrude swore there was a swarm of bees under her bed and had all the gardeners up with smoke and things. She refused to get out of bed until the bees were gone — and there weren't any there. And then there was the time grandfather made a wreath of strawberry-leaves and danced round the garden singing 'Cook's son, Dook's son, son of a belted earl.' It didn't strike me at the time, but that was an odd thing to do, wasn't it? Anyway, I shan't see them again for months and months. Oh, Ernest, it's too wonderful. You don't think the sleeves are too tight, do you? Are people black in Athens?"

"Not coal black — mostly Jews and undergraduates."

"What's that?"

"Well, Peter's an undergraduate. I was one until a few weeks ago."

"I say, do you think people will take me for an undergraduate?"

IV

It seems to me sometimes that Nature, like a lazy author, will round off abruptly into a short story what she obviously intended to be the opening of a novel.

Two letters arrived for me by the post next morning. One was from my bank returning the Duke's cheque for £150 marked "Payment Stopped"; the other from a firm of solicitors enjoining me that they, or rather one of them, would call upon me that morning in connection with the Duke of Vanburgh's business. I took them in to George.

All he said was: "I had a sort of feeling that this was all too good to last."

The lawyer duly arrived. He seemed displeased that neither of us was dressed. He intimated that he wished to speak to me alone.

His Grace, he said, had altered his plans for his grandson. He no longer wished him to go abroad. Of course, between ourselves we had to admit that the boy was not quite sane . . . very sad . . . these old families . . . putting me in such a difficult position in case anything happened. . . . His Grace had talked it over with Lady Emily and Lady Gertrude. . . . It really was too dangerous an experiment . . . besides, they had especially kept the boy shut away because they did not want the world to know . . . discredit on a great name . . . and, of course, if he went about, people were bound to talk. It was not strictly his business to discuss the wisdom of his client's decisions, but, again between ourselves, he had been very much surprised that his Grace had ever considered letting the boy leave home. . . . Later perhaps, but not yet . . . he would always need watching. And of course there was a good deal of money coming to him. Strictly between ourselves, his Grace was a great deal better off than people supposed . . . town property . . . death duties . . . keeping up Stayle . . . and so on.

He was instructed to pay the expenses incurred up to date and to give me three months' salary . . . most generous of his Grace, no legal obligation. . . . As to the clothes . . . we really seemed rather to have exceeded his Grace's instructions. Still, no doubt all the things that had not been specially made could be returned to the shops. He would give instructions about that . . . he was himself to take Lord Stayle back to his grandfather.

And an hour later they left.

"It's been a marvellous four days," said George; and then: "Anyway, I shall be twenty-one in three years and I shall have my mother's money then. I think it's rather a shame sending back those ties though. Don't you think I could keep one or two?"

Five minutes later Julia rang up to ask us to luncheon.

"Did you ever hear of him again?"

The question was Miss Pogson's. But before Mr. Butterworth could answer the Courier broke in with:

"Indefensible!—Monstrous! These stately homes of England! Bah! I thank God I am of the proletariat. I heard of another experience like that, too. Even more demoralising—if that's possible."

Henry Scott chuckled.

"You have not, my friend, the ducal point of view. It takes the accumulation of many centuries to acquire. It is a point of view as unalterable as the Calendar, and as baffling as—as what we will call

THE FIFTH DAY'S TALE OF THE PSYCHIC RESEARCHER"

Appendix   Boiling the Pot and Playing the Poet

38

The Manager of "The Kremlin"

[Although Waugh's novels were relatively successful even in his early years, he depended upon ephemeral journalism for a substantial part of his income. Depending on his bank balance, he could be accommodating or distant. To judge from *Catalogue*, E121, which asks his agent about the possibility of payment in advance, he needed the money rather badly and was not at all ashamed to take it for minor work. *Vile Bodies* had just been published, but it was not established as a hit, and contracts from the daily press had not begun to arrive at his agent's. Text: *John Bull* 47 (February 15, 1930): 22, 24, in the series "Real Life Stories—by Famous Authors," illustrated by Herbert Hyde. Reprinted, *Daily Herald*, October 22, 1937, pp. 18, 22.]

This story was told me in Paris very early in the morning by the manager of a famous night club, and I am fairly certain that it is true.

I shall not tell you the real name of the manager or of his club, because it is not the sort of advertisement he would like, but I will call them, instead, Boris and "The Kremlin."

"The Kremlin" occupies a position of its own.

Your hat and coat are taken at the door by a perfectly genuine Cossack of ferocious appearance; he wears riding-boots and spurs, and the parts of his face that are not hidden by beard are cut and scarred like that of a pre-war German student.

The interior is hung with rugs and red, woven stuff to represent a tent. There is a very good *tsigain* band playing gipsy music, and a very good jazz-band which plays when people want to dance.

The waiters are chosen for their height. They wear magnificent Russian liveries, and carry round flaming skewers on which are spitted onions between rounds of meat. Most of them are ex-officers of the Imperial Guard.

Boris, the manager, is quite a young man; he is 6 ft. 5½ in. in height. He wears a Russian silk blouse, loose trousers and top boots, and goes from table to table seeing that everything is all right.

From two in the morning until dawn "The Kremlin" is invariably full, and the American visitors, looking wistfully at their bills, often remark that Boris must be "making a good thing out of it." So he is.

Fashions change very quickly in Montmartre, but if his present popularity lasts for another season, he talks of retiring to a villa on the Riviera.

One Saturday night, or rather a Sunday morning, Boris did me the honour of coming to sit at my table and take a glass of wine with me. It was then that Boris told his story.

His father was a general, and when the war broke out Boris was a cadet at the military academy.

He was too young to fight, and was forced to watch, from behind the lines, the collapse of the Imperial Government.

Then came the confused period when the Great War was over, and various scattered remnants of the royalist army, with half hearted support from their former allies, were engaged in a losing fight against the Bolshevists.

Boris was eighteen years old. His father had been killed and his mother had already escaped to America.

The military academy was being closed down, and with several of his fellow cadets Boris decided to join the last royalist army which, under Kolchak, was holding the Bolshevists at bay in Siberia.

It was a very odd kind of army. There were dismounted cavalry and sailors who had left their ships, officers whose regiments had mutinied, frontier garrisons and aides-de-camp, veterans of the Russo-Japanese war, and boys like Boris who were seeing action for the first time.

Besides these, there were units from the Allied Powers, who seemed to have been sent there by their capricious Governments and forgotten; there was a corps of British engineers and some French artillery; there were also liaison officers and military attachés to the General Headquarters Staff.

Among the latter was a French cavalry officer a few years older than Boris. To most educated Russians before the war French was as familiar as their own language.

Boris and the French attaché became close friends. They used to smoke together and talk of Moscow and Paris before the war.

As the weeks passed it became clear that Kolchak's campaign could end in nothing but disaster.

Eventually a council of officers decided that the only course open was to break through to the east coast and attempt to escape to Europe.

A force had to be left behind to cover the retreat, and Boris and his French friend found themselves detailed to remain with this rearguard. In the action which followed, the small covering force was completely routed.

Alone among the officers Boris and his friend escaped with their lives, but their condition was almost desperate.

Their baggage was lost and they found themselves isolated in a waste land, patrolled by enemy troops and inhabited by savage Asiatic tribesmen.

Left to himself, the Frenchman's chances of escape were negligible, but a certain prestige still attached to the uniform of a Russian officer in the outlying villages.

Boris lent him his military overcoat to cover his uniform, and together they struggled through the snow, begging their way to the frontier.

Eventually they arrived in Japanese territory. Here all Russians were suspect, and it devolved on the Frenchman to get them safe conduct to the nearest French Consulate.

Boris' chief aim now was to join his mother in America. His friend had to return to report himself in Paris, so here they parted.

They took an affectionate farewell, promising to see each other again when their various affairs were settled. But each in his heart doubted whether chance would ever bring them together again.

Two years elapsed, and then one day in spring a poorly-dressed young Russian found himself in Paris, with three hundred francs in his pocket and all his worldly possessions in a kitbag.

He was very different from the debonair Boris who had left the military academy for Kolchak's army. America had proved to be something very different from the Land of Opportunity he had imagined.

His mother sold the jewels and a few personal possessions she had been able to bring away with her, and had started a small dressmaking business.

There seemed no chance of permanent employment for Boris, so after two or three months of casual jobs he worked his passage to England.

During the months that followed, Boris obtained temporary employment as a waiter, a chauffeur, a professional dancing-partner, a dock-labourer, and he came very near to starvation.

Finally, he came across an old friend of his father's, a former first secretary in the diplomatic corps, who was now working as a hairdresser.

This friend advised him to try Paris, where a large Russian colony had already formed, and gave him his fare.

It was thus that one morning, as the buds were just beginning to break in the Champs Elysées and the *couturiers* were exhibiting their Spring fashions, Boris found himself, ill-dressed and friendless, in another strange city.

His total capital was the equivalent of about thirty shillings; and so, being uncertain of what was to become of him, he decided to have luncheon.

An Englishman finding himself in this predicament would no doubt have made careful calculations.

He would have decided what was the longest time that his money would last him, and would have methodically kept within his budget while he started again "looking for a job."

But as Boris stood working out this depressing sum, something seemed suddenly to snap in his head.

With the utmost privation he could hardly hope to subsist for more than two or three weeks.

At the end of that time he would be in exactly the same position, a fortnight older, with all his money spent and no nearer a job.

Why not now as well as in a fortnight's time? He was in Paris, about which he had read and heard so much. He made up his mind to have one good meal and leave the rest to chance.

He had often heard his father speak of a restaurant called Larne. He had no idea where it was, so he took a taxi.

He entered the restaurant and sat down in one of the red-plush seats, while the waiters eyed his clothes with suspicion.

He looked about him in an unembarrassed way. It was quieter and less showy in appearance than the big restaurants he had passed in New York and London, but a glance at the menu told him that it was not a place where poor people often went.

Then he began ordering his luncheon, and the waiter's manner quickly changed as he realised that this eccentrically dressed customer did not need any advice about choosing his food and wine.

He ate fresh caviare and *ortolansan porto* and *crepes suzettes*; he drank a bottle of vintage claret and a glass of very old *fine champagne*, and he examined several boxes of cigars before he found one in perfect condition.

When he had finished, he asked for his bill. It was 260 francs. He gave the waiter a tip of 26 francs and 4 francs to the man at the door who had taken his hat and kit-bag. His taxi had cost 7 francs.

Half a minute later he stood on the kerb with exactly 3 francs in the world. But it had been a magnificent lunch, and he did not regret it.

As he stood there, meditating what he could do, his arm was suddenly taken from behind, and turning he saw a smartly dressed Frenchman, who had evidently just left the restaurant. It was his friend the military attaché.

"I was sitting at the table behind you," he said. "You never noticed me, you were so intent on your food."

"It is probably my last meal for some time," Boris explained, and his friend laughed at what he took to be a joke.

They walked up the street together, talking rapidly. The Frenchman described how he had left the army when his time of service was up, and was now a director of a prosperous motor business.

"And you, too," he said. "I am delighted to see that you also have been doing well."

"Doing well? At the moment I have exactly 3 francs in the world."

"My dear fellow, people with 3 francs in the world do not eat caviare at Larne."

Then for the first time he noticed Boris' frayed clothes. He had only known him in a war-worn uniform and it had seemed natural at first to find him dressed as he was.

Now he realised that these were not the clothes which prosperous young men usually wear.

"My dear friend," he said, "forgive me for laughing. I didn't realise. . . . Come and dine with me this evening at my flat, and we will talk about what is to be done."

"And so," concluded Boris, "I became the manager of 'The Kremlin.' *If I had not gone to Larne that day it is about certain we should never have met!*

"My friend said that I might have a part in his motor business, but that he thought anyone who could spend his last 300 francs on one meal was ordained by God to keep a restaurant.

"So it has been. He financed me. I collected some of my old friends to work with us. Now, you see, I am comparatively a rich man."

The last visitors had paid their bill and risen, rather unsteadily, to go. Boris rose, too, to bow them out. The daylight shone into the room as they lifted the curtain to go out.

Suddenly, in the new light, all the decorations looked bogus and tawdry; the waiters hurried away to change their sham liveries. Boris understood what I was feeling.

"I know," he said. "It is not Russian. It is not anything even to own a popular night club when one has lost one's country."

39

Juvenilia

[This poem, mentioned nowhere in Waugh's diaries or *Letters*, was published as the tenth impression of *Vile Bodies* was being issued and *Labels* was being serialized. Waugh was writing regular features for the *Daily Mail* and a book-review column for the *Graphic*. Text: *Farrago* (Oxford), no. 2 (June, 1930): 88.]

I

Tritely I said, "your love like grateful rain
Soothes my dried heart and bids it grow again."
Such drops, I think, as, other curtains drawn,
Woke other lovers at another dawn,
Moistened hot brows and cooled their sweating shanks
While Noah chopped and Japheth banged the planks.

II

Evelyn, like Brutus, with himself at war
Forgets no show of love. Heidseik '04
Marshals him on and wakes the old response
To satisfy Lucasta's simple wants;
And Château Yquem tho' the taste be gall
Moves the machine to acts mechanical.

40

Too Much Tolerance

[Waugh interrupted the composition of *Black Mischief* to write this story, part 7 of the series "The Seven Deadly Sins of Today," and some other short stories and film dialogue, for ready money. When first approached about the series, he told his agent that he had not decided on which sin to treat and could not put it on a post card anyway. He agreed to write the story on February 26, announced his topic about March 18, and delivered the manuscript of the introduction about March 20 with a note saying that he was still not sure what was wanted (see *Catalogue*, E173–77). For Waugh's introduction to the story, see "Tolerance," *John Bull*, April 2, 1932, p. 7. Reprinted in *The Essays, Articles, and Reviews of Evelyn Waugh*, ed. Donat Gallagher (London: Methuen, 1983), p. 128. Text: *John Bull*, May 21, 1932, pp. 22–24.]

A round, amiable face, reddened rather than browned by the tropical sun; round, rather puzzled grey eyes; close-cut sandy hair; a large, smiling mouth; a small sandy moustache; clean white duck suit and sun helmet—a typical English commercial agent stopping between ships at a stifling little port on the Red Sea.

We were the only Europeans in the hotel. The boat for which we were both waiting was two days late. We spent all our time together.

We went round the native bazaar and played interminable games of poker dice at the café tables. In these circumstances a casual acquaintance easily assumes a confidential tone.

At first naturally enough we talked of general subjects—local conditions and race problems.

"Can't understand what all the trouble's about. They're all jolly chaps when you get to know them." British officials, traders, Arabs, natives, Indian settlers—they were all to my new friend jolly good chaps.

Such an odd thing they couldn't get on better. Of course, different races had different ideas—some didn't wash, some had queer ideas about honesty, some got out of hand at times when they'd had too much to drink.

"Still," he said, "that's nobody's business but their own. If only they'd all let each other alone to go their own ways there wouldn't be any problems. As for religions, well, there was a lot of good in them all—Hindu, Mahommedan, Pagan; the missionaries did a lot of good, too—Wesleyan, Catholic, Church of England, all jolly good fellows."

People in remote parts of the world tend to have unshakable views on every topic. After a few months spent among them it was a relief to come across so tolerant and broad a mind.

On the first evening I left my companion with a feeling of warm respect. Here at last, in a continent peopled almost exclusively by fanatics of one kind of another, I thought I had found a nice man.

Next day we got on to more intimate subjects and I began to learn something of his life. He was now nearer fifty than forty years of age, though I should have thought him younger.

He had been an only son, brought up in an English provincial town in a household where rigid principles of Victorian decorum dominated its members.

He had been born late in his parents' life, and all his memories dated from after his father's retirement from a responsible Government post in India.

It was alien to his nature to admit the existence of discomfort or disagreement, but it was clear from his every reference to it that his home had not been a congenial one.

Exact rules of morals and etiquette, ruthless criticism of neighbours, an insurmountable class-barrier raised against all who were considered socially inferior, hostile disapproval of superiors—these were clearly the code of my friend's parents, and he had grown up with a deep-rooted resolution to model his own life on opposite principles.

I had been surprised on the evening of our first meeting to discover the nature of his work. He was engaged in selling sewing-machines on commission to Indian store-keepers up and down the East African coast.

It was clearly not the job for which his age and education should have fitted him. Later I learned the explanation.

He had gone into business on leaving his public school, had done quite well, and eventually, just before the war, had set up on his own with the capital left him at his father's death.

"I had bad luck there," he said. "I never feel quite to blame over what happened. You see, I'd taken a chap into partnership with me. He'd been a clerk with me in the office, and I'd always liked him, though he didn't get on very well with the other fellows.

"He got sacked just about the time I came in for some money. I never quite made out what the trouble was about, and anyway it was none of my business. The arrangement seemed rather lucky at first, because my partner wasn't fit for military service, so all the time I was in the army he was able to look after things at home.

"The business seemed to be going very well, too. We moved to new offices and took on a larger staff, and all through the war we were drawing very decent dividends. But apparently it was only temporary prosperity.

"When I got back after the Armistice I didn't pay a great deal of attention to my affairs, I'm afraid. I was glad to be home and wanted to make the most of peace. I left my partner to manage everything and I suppose I more or less let things slide for two years.

"Anyway I didn't know how bad things were until he suddenly told me that we should have to go into liquidation.

"Since then I've been lucky in getting jobs, but it isn't quite the same as being one's own master."

He gazed out across the quay, turning his glass idly in his hand. then, as an after-thought, he made an illuminating addition to his story.

"One thing I'm very glad of," he said, "my partner didn't come down with me. Almost immediately after we closed down he opened on his own in the same way of business on quite a large scale. He's a rich man now."

Later in the day he surprised me by casually mentioning his son.
"Son?"

"Yes, I've a boy of twenty-seven at home. Awfully nice fellow. I wish I could get back more often to see him. But he's got his own friends now and I dare say he's happy by himself. He's interested in the theatre.

"It's not a thing I know much about myself. All his friends are theatrical, you know, jolly interesting.

"I'm glad the boy has struck out for himself. I always made a point of never trying to force his interest in anything that didn't attract him.

"The only pity is that there's very little money in it. He's always hoping to get a job either on the stage or the kinema, but it's difficult if you don't know the right people, he says, and that's expensive.

"I send him as much as I can, but he has to be well dressed, you know, and go about a good deal and entertain, and all that takes money. Still, I expect it'll lead to something in the end. He's a jolly good fellow."

But it was not until some days later, on board ship, when we were already berthed at the port where he was due to disembark next day, that he mentioned his wife.

We had had many drinks to wish each other good luck on our respective journeys. The prospect of immediate separation made mutual confidence easier than it would be between constant companions.

"My wife left me," he said simply. "It was a great surprise. I can't to this day think why. I always encouraged her to do just what she wanted.

"You see, I'd seen a lot of the Victorian idea of marriage, where a wife was supposed to have no interests outside her housekeeping, and the father of the family dined at home every evening. I don't approve of that.

"I always liked my wife to have her own friends and have them in the house when she wanted and to go out when she wanted, and I did the same. I thought we were ideally happy.

"She liked dancing and I didn't, so when a chap turned up who she seemed to like going about with, I was delighted. I'd met him once or twice and heard that he ran after women a good bit, but that wasn't my business.

"My father used to keep a strict division among his friends, between those he saw at home and those he met in the club. He wouldn't bring anyone to his house whose moral character he didn't wholly approve of. I think that's all old-fashioned rot.

"Anyway, to cut a long story short, after she'd been going out with this fellow for some time she suddenly fell in love and went off with him. I'd always liked him, too. Jolly good sort of fellow. I suppose she had a perfect right to do what she preferred. All the same, I was surprised. And I've been lonely since."

At this moment two fellow-passengers whose acquaintance I had been scrupulously avoiding came past our table. He called them to our table, so I wished him "Good-night" and went below.

I did not see him to speak to next day, but I caught a brief glimpse of him on the pier, supervising the loading of his crate of sample sewing-machines.

As I watched, he finished his business and strode off towards the town—a jaunty, tragic little figure, cheated out of his patrimony by his partner, battened on by an obviously worthless son, deserted by his wife, an irrepressible, bewildered figure striding off under his bobbing topee, cheerfully butting his way into a whole continent of rapacious and ruthless jolly good fellows.

41

The Sympathetic Passenger

[This story was written just after Waugh completed *Mexico: An Object Lesson* and just before he began work on what was to become *Work Suspended*. Waugh agreed on April 15 to write the story; it was being typed on April 25. He told his agent that it might make a good short film, but nothing came of the suggestion. *Catalogue*, E366, 368–69. Text: *Daily Mail*, May 4, 1939, p. 4.]

As Mr. James shut the side door behind him, radio music burst from every window of his house. Agnes, in the kitchen, was tuned in to one station; his wife, washing her hair in the bathroom, to another.

The competing programmes followed him to the garage and into the lane.

He had twelve miles to drive to the station, and for the first five of them he remained in a black mood.

He was in most matters a mild-tempered person — in all matters, it might be said, except one; he abominated the wireless.

It was not merely that it gave him no pleasure; it gave active pain, and, in the course of years, he had come to regard the invention as being directed deliberately against himself, a conspiracy of his enemies to disturb and embitter what should have been the placid last years of his life.

He was far from being an old man; he was, in fact, in his middle fifties; he had retired young, almost precipitously, as soon as a small legacy had made it possible. He had been a lover of quiet all his life.

Mrs. James did not share this preference.

Now they were settled in a small country house, twelve miles from a suitable cinema.

The wireless, for Mrs. James, was a link with the clean pavements and bright shop windows, a communion with millions of fellow beings.

Mr. James saw it in just that light too. It was what he minded most — the violation of his privacy. He brooded with growing resentment on the vulgarity of womankind.

In this mood he observed a burly man of about his own age signalling to him for a lift from the side of the road. He stopped.

"I wonder if by any chance you are going to the railway station?" The man spoke politely with a low, rather melancholy voice.

"I am; I have to pick up a parcel. Jump in."

"That's very kind of you."

The man took his place beside Mr. James. His boots were dusty, and he sank back in his seat as though he had come from far and was weary.

He had very large, ugly hands, close-cut grey hair, a bony, rather sunken face.

For a mile or so he did not speak. Then he asked suddenly, "Has this car got a wireless?"

"Certainly not."

"What is that knob for?" He began examining the dashboard. "And that?"

"One is the self-starter. That other is supposed to light cigarettes. It does not work. If," he continued sharply, "you have stopped me in the hope of hearing the wireless, I can only suggest that I put you down and let you try your luck on someone else."

"Heaven forbid," said his passenger. "I detest the thing."

"So do I."

"Sir, you are one among millions. I regard myself as highly privileged in making your acquaintance."

"Thank you. It is a beastly invention."

The passenger's eyes glowed with passionate sympathy. "It is worse. It is diabolical."

"Very true."

"Literally diabolical. It is put here by the devil to destroy us. Did you know that it spread the most terrible diseases?"

"I didn't know it. But I can well believe it."

"It causes cancer, tuberculosis, infantile paralysis, and the common cold. I have proved it."

"It certainly causes headaches," said Mr. James.

"No man," said his passenger, "has suffered more excruciating headaches than I.

"They have tried to kill me with headaches. But I was too clever for them. Did you know that the B.B.C. has its own prisons, its own torture chambers?"

"I have long suspected it."

"I know. I have experienced them. Now it is the time of revenge."

Mr. James glanced rather uneasily at his passenger and drove a little faster.

"I have a plan," continued the big man. "I am going to London to put it into execution. I am going to kill the Director-General. I shall kill them *all*."

They drove on in silence. They were nearing the outskirts of the town when a larger car driven by a girl drew abreast of them and passed. From inside it came the unmistakable sounds of a jazz band. The big man sat up in his seat, rigid as a pointer.

"Do you hear that?" he said. "*She's* got one. After, her, *quick*."

"No good," said Mr. James. "We can never catch that car."

"We can try. We *shall* try, unless," he said with a new and more sinister note in his voice, "unless you don't want to."

Mr. James accelerated. But the large car was nearly out of sight.

"Once before," said his passenger, "I was tricked. The B.B.C. sent out one of their spies. He was very like you. He pretended to be one of my followers; he said he was taking me to the Director-General's office. Instead he took me to a prison. Now I know what to do with spies. I kill them." He leaned towards Mr. James.

"I assure you, my dear sir, you have no more loyal supporter than myself. It is simply a question of cars. I cannot overtake her. But no doubt we shall find her at the station."

"We shall see. If we do not, I shall know whom to thank, and how to thank him."

They were in the town now and making for the station. Mr. James looked despairingly at the policeman on point duty, but was signalled on with a negligent flick on the hand. In the station yard the passenger looked round eagerly.

"I do not see that car," he said.

Mr. James fumbled for a second with the catch of the door and then tumbled out. "Help!" he cried. "Help! There's a madman here."

With a great shout of anger the man dodged round the front of the car and bore down on him.

At the moment three men in uniforms charged out of the station doorway. There was a brief scuffle; then, adroitly, they had their man strapped up.

"We thought he'd make for the railway," said their chief. "You must have had quite an exciting drive, sir."

Mr. James could scarcely speak. "Wireless," he muttered weakly.

"Ho, he's been talking to you about that, has he? Then you're very lucky to be here to tell us. It's his foible, as you might say. I hope you didn't disagree with him."

"No," said Mr. James, "At least, not at first."

"Well, you're luckier than some. He can't be crossed, not about wireless. Gets very wild. Why, he killed two people and half killed a third last time he got away. Well, many thanks for bringing him in so nicely, sir. We must be getting him home."

Home. Mr. James drove back along the familiar road.

"Why," said his wife when he entered the house. "How quick you've been. Where's the parcel?"

"I think I must have forgotten it."

"How very unlike you. Why, you're looking quite ill. I'll run in and tell Agnes to switch off the radio. She can't have heard you come in."

"No," said Mr. James, sitting down heavily. "Not switch off radio. Like it. Homely."